For Margaret — with thanks for listening.

Good Gothe!

The Enthusiasms of an Airwave Connoisseur

[signature]

Jurgen Gothe

London

24 OCT 90

Stoddart

Kate gets this one –
she's already got everything else

Copyright © 1990 by Jurgen Gothe

First published in 1990 by
Stoddart Publishing Co. Limited
34 Lesmill Road
Toronto, Canada
M3B 2T6

CANADIAN CATALOGUING IN PUBLICATION DATA

Gothe, Jurgen, 1944-
  Good gothe!

ISBN 0-7737-2292-0

I. Title.

PS8563.0844G6 1990   C818'.54   C90-094655-5
PR9199.3.G677G6 1990

Typesetting: Tony Gordon Ltd.
Printed in Canada

Many of these pieces have appeared, if somewhat differently in some cases, in the following publications: The Victoria Times-Colonist, Western Living Magazine, The BCLDB Guide, Wine Tidings Magazine, Fugue Magazine, The Financial Post Magazine, Epicure Magazine, Easy Living Magazine, The Vancouver Province, enRoute Magazine, Canadian Lawyer Magazine, Kanata Magazine, The First Vancouver Catalogue, The National Radio Guide, and on CBC Stereo, CBC Radio, CHQM-FM, and C-FAX.

"Sphinx and Cheops and Ted and Alice and Puss and Boots" first appeared in Workman Publications' "Cat Catalog," published in 1976 in New York. The two go-to-sleep stories haven't appeared anywhere before except over a few sleeping heads . . .

Contents

PART TWO

Life with the Cats

PART THREE

Jogging with Beethoven

Acknowledgements

———————— ❧ ————————

THANKS A LOT, eh!

Karen Brown for all the right stuff. You know the bit about "without whom this would never have been possible"? Well, it wouldn't have been, either . . .

Denise Bukowski for inventing it and being all those things a good agent should be and, no, I'm not listing them here . . .

Will Peacock for the computer-taming and all that wonderful stuff that's in there I don't understand. Don Munro for bringing the computer in the first place. I think . . .

All the editors who ever took pencil to any of this and wouldn't give up before it was nearly readable, but most especially Shaun Oakey for stylish, skilful, sympathetic, and painless editing. I know, I know – a few of those adjectives could come out without hurting the flow, but this is *my* page . . .

Sandra Hooymans and Melissa Blaney for inputting at the damndest hours. Is that how you spell *inputting*?

Rob Charlton for legalese and wine; Don Bastian and Nelson Doucet for lunch and what came with it; Bill Phillips for all those mysterious gyroscopes; Carol Munro for Carol Munro.

The DiscDrive crew for keeping me in sound shape, 3 to 6, Monday to Friday, coast to coast.

Millie Shapiro for "Woman with Two Cats" and one with one.

All those wine makers and music makers, for all the goodies; and all the veterinarians for keeping The Cats in tune.

Marilyn Janis, first keeper of The Cats; Pat Sloan, of course – and the Willis Point Fire Department; Marilyn McLean, just because.

And of course, that first hydrogen atom, billions and billions of years ago, for starting the ball rolling . . .

Introduction

---

*S*O SANTA WASN'T A BIG LOSS; I mean, what? Large guy in red and white – those colors may be okay on a flag but a guy's clothes? Anyway, he only came 'round once a year and extracted a lot of unreasonable promises before giving you anything; so that whole thing wasn't a problem

But having to go to work . . .??? Yikes!

So one very hot summer in Medicine Hat, as proud owner of a '54 Monarch with a moon roof and banana-rolled green-and-yellow leather seats (I could use that now, for jacket material!), making sewer pipes for a living for the Medicine Hat Brick & Tile, I decided the whole thing wasn't working. Not that there's anything wrong with sewer pipes; someone has to make them and imagine the kind of world we'd be in if they didn't. But it was hard work and hot and the pay wasn't hot and the sandwiches melted in the lunch box and I thought I'd be better to try to make a living by my wits, or better still, my senses. Was that sensible?

That sort of question never bothered me before; didn't then, doesn't now. But the typewriter came out from under the bed and there was a copywriting job at the Voice of the Gas City, CHAT, and then there was an on-air shift one New Year's Eve because nobody else wanted to do it and something got published in a paper and then there was a magazine piece and, finally, enough money to take the train out to the West Coast and pursue this broadcaster-journalist thing seriously.

Sort of.

Trouble was, people wanted stuff written about Important Issues. Now, I recognize that Important Issues are important as much as the next guy does. But there are enough people writing importantly and analysing the I.I.'s and interpreting the facts and I think that's fine.

I didn't think, though, there were enough people writing about wine and food and music and cats. So I thought I would try to fill the wine and food and music and cats gap (WAFAMACG, as it's known in Official Circles).

I'll tell you what it's like. It's a little like being a dermatologist, I think – though I've never been one. But you get the perks of being a doctor except nobody calls you at two-thirty in the morning to deliver babies. Not that there's anything wrong with delivering babies at two-thirty in the morning; someone has to do it and imagine the kind of world we'd live in if they didn't.

So I get to write more or less what I like *about* what I like and I get a press card, which sometimes keeps my car from being towed away from in front of wineries, if they happen to be downtown. And I get to travel and talk to people and make a living writing about what some of my senses are into – taste and smell and sight and sound. If I could just get a gig writing a massage column, somewhere . . .

The nice thing is nobody sends me to get shot at. That I do all by myself; just to show you that we're talking intrepid in the line of duty I can proudly claim to be the only Canadian wine writer to visit Lebanon's Château Musar during the time people *were* shooting.

Food came first; I ate before I drank wine. But once I discovered wine there was no stopping. The cats showed up around the same time and the music was always there. I kind of like it this way; it keeps me entertained. I hope you do, too.

The difficulty with this collection is what we had to leave out.

Like lunch! There was going to be a food section as well: recipes, first-roast-chicken-of-the-fall stories, tales of judging zucchini carvings in Hong Kong; airline-kitchen secrets; Ten Favorite Restaurants Around the World; where the world's best crème brûlée is; and a lot of restaurant memories from seven or eight thousand different eateries on most of the continents, lo these last thirty years. But there wasn't room and the publishers wanted to keep the price of the book under $37.50, so we will have to do those another time, if you're interested.

So this, then, is for all those people who enjoy my wine ramblings over Sunday brunch in Victoria or share a flight with me, reading about a dinner, or who file away my restaurant recommendations after coming across them six months old in the waiting room of their dentist's office or who thumb through music and recordings commentary with me at Towers or Sam's or who discover a couple of neat backroads wineries in Sonoma as a result of a piece I've all but forgotten writing for an Asian journal and all the rest.

But mostly it's for all those people who spend the afternoons with me, letting me drive a few discs and talk about Mozart's shoes and what's for dinner with the cats cooking and the fact it happens to be St. Furbish Day.

You're great company for somebody who's stuck in CBC Radio's subterranean Studio 20 in downtown Vancouver three hours a day.

PART ONE

Travels with My Wineglass

Wine for the Fun of It

————————— ❦ —————————

ALL RIGHT, THEN, let's *be* radical, right off the bat: wine is No Big Deal! It's meant to be drunk, enjoyed, remembered fondly, if the pot roast it went with was one of those fabulous Italian numbers with the little pockets of fresh herbs and garlic. But above all, wine is meant to be poured: (a) in a glass and (b) down the throat.

There's really nothing much to wine. Nature makes it without a lot of fuss. It's only when people get into the act that things gets complicated.

Wine isn't something to hang on the wall and stare at. It's not something to get all poetic about — unless you happen to be a poet and do that sort of thing in your daily line of work. When somebody tells me that I'm not enjoying a simple, natural drink but having a transcendental experience, I'm out the door by the third adjective!

Let's just experience wine first. Then, if there's time and anything left in the bottle, we'll get around to transcending something!

The only way to learn anything about wine is to drink it. The more you taste, the more you can compare. Comparison is the best approach. Wine books do that sometimes, but they're not always much help. They often assume that that you have a lot of

3

knowledge and take off from there. Besides, many wine writers love the putdown above all else. It's fashionable — and easier — to come up with a snappy line about a wine's shortcomings than to say a few selective things about what makes it good.

Wine prose can be some of the silliest in the language. If you really care that the wine recalls a burst of lilac on the front palate, reminiscences of marigolds in leather, encrustations of vanilla-lemon on a field of fleurs-de-lis with civets rampant, don't read on; browse among the greeting cards at the corner drugstore. Or get one of those new books that surface every season, in which the pompous shed purple prose like cat fur.

Back to something radical: wine *is* fun. A lot of people won't let it be; they mull and stew and sip and mutter and leave us confused and half-convinced it's not quite as good as we thought and anyway, it doesn't hold a candle to the private reserve made just after the war by the wine maker's nine-year-old for show-and-tell.

We learn about wine by tasting. Tasting is subjective. That means your personal opinion is just as valid as Hugh Johnson's. He may have a few thousand bottles' more experience than you, but that doesn't make his opinions any more valid, merely broader based.

So the only way to do it is to do it. But how to start? I've never found any good beginners' seminars to attend. The way to start is by following this little personal guide to help make the journey more enjoyable.

There's more enjoyment in numbers, so do it with friends. This isn't solitaire; it's more like bridge, or better yet, hearts. The more the merrier. Not to mention easier on your budget.

The wine world is bewildering but only because there is so much to choose from. Regardless of where you jump in, after the first few sessions you're on your way to enjoyment. Half a dozen good friends; a few tastings planned around dinners, picnics, outings; a visit to a wine festival; a tasting tour of a winery or three — that's the ticket.

Don't worry about doing it right or wrong. There are preferred methods, and most of them are based on something rational. You'll get to know them. But the first approach is simplicity itself: open a bottle, get some glasses, pour the wine.

Do keep notes. That's the important thing. Write your impressions (and the name of the wine, the year, the price) in a little notebook you can take with you to tastings and stores. Soak the labels off the bottles and put them in a scrapbook along with your comments. Let everybody write in their comments as well. (If you have trouble soaking the labels off bottles — some seem fused to the glass — find out the name of the agent and ask if they could send you a couple of new ones. Many — but not all — keep extras.)

Start keeping score. Grudgingly, I'm giving in to the point system that Robert Parker has foisted on the world. There *is* something to be said for rating wines out of a hundred points. Anyway, you can't beat 'em, so join 'em — it's the going trend.

The only reservation I have about the 100-point scale is that it can cut you off from pleasant experiences if you put too much store in it. It's still a matter of someone else's taste and taste buds you're listening to. If a Parkerite says it's 91 and sensational, by all means try it. But don't avoid a wine rated at 75 just because of the number. Taste it yourself. You might like it.

And that's a key point: you drink what you like. It's *your* money — *you* choose. Everybody talks dry, dry, dry. Truth is, most people — even some of the most vocal sophisticated palates — like a lot of their wines sweet. At any wine festival, what is everybody starstruck by? The late harvests, the German dessert wines, that amazing Tokaji Essencia from Hungary that is so sweet you can pour it on ice cream. Sure, people *talk* bone-dry Sauvignons and lean-edged Zinfandels. But they gulp the stickies!

If you like them, drink them. If you don't, leave them alone. If red wine gives you a headache, avoid it. If white gives you heartburn, stay away. If champagne makes your eyes water, launch your boat with vermouth!

5

It's a good idea to plan your wine journey according to country or region, wine variety, prices, the season — just about any theme. Spring is a nice time for the full-flavored whites, the Chardonnays and such. Later in the summer, the sparklers then, light whites, the kind you cut with soda and lime. In the fall, lighter red wines, and in the winter, the big bruisers: classic wines such as Cabernet and dessert wines. That's the direction to take.

What about wine clubs and societies? Best idea is to start your own impromptu group. If you have a club already — travelling dinner group, bridge club, service club branch, ski buddies, professional society, even your strata council! — you might canvass the membership to see who's interested.

There are many wine societies around, but it's a matter of finding the right one. Some are stuffy and stodgy and others are pompous; a few have fun. Where are they? Ask the consulates or trade commissions of the various wine-producing countries. Australia, France, Germany, Italy, Spain, the United States — they can all put you in touch with their wine groups. And persevere — some may give you a brushoff. Most will be delighted to help, though. They *are* here to market their countries' products, after all.

When you get in touch with the societies, find out if they have new-member tastings or if you can "audit" one of their events to see how it feels to you. No point committing yourself to a membership (they usually cost something) to learn you're going to be bored or way out of your depth for a year.

As well, contact some of the agents or wine company representatives. Many have extensive wine portfolios and staff who know — and love — wines. The Yellow Pages aren't a bad place to start looking, or get in touch with import vintners' associations and ask if they can let you have a list of members. Call one or two and ask for a product list.

You will find that most agents, and even wine writers and educators, are happy to talk to your group. Some charge, most don't; ask first. Schedules are often tight, so you may have to do some calendar juggling. Indicate your level of wine awareness and ask if a tasting can be arranged. Agents are interested in selling their own wines, of course, so there may be a bias, though most of them will be glad to cover the basics of their particular corner of the wine world.

It's fun to experiment with wine at the dinner table, either at home or in a restaurant. Some restaurant wine lists are reliable and the staff trustworthy, some aren't — not because they don't want to help you with your wine choice but rather because until recently there hasn't been much interest in wine service in Canada. I'm happy to say that's all changing.

If you start your own neighborhood society, incorporate a food focus. Matching wines to foods is a satisfying pastime: French food with fine châteaux or hearty vins du pays; tapas with dollar-conscious Riojas; California cuisine with buttery Chardonnays; Mexican dinners . . . well, there is always tequila with a Corona chaser!

This kind of experimenting makes even a simple meal an event. After all, someone had to come up with the first pairing of Pinot Noir and Brie, or Stilton and Porto, or Chablis with oysters. Some surprises seem logical if you consider them: Sherry with consommé? Why not? Many chefs put it in the soup; no reason why you can't serve it alongside, good and chilled.

Voyaging through wine is like taking a little holiday — sometimes it's fun to go where you haven't been before. Try the new wines from Israel. You may not like them, but at least you will have "been there." You might end up loving them, and then you can go back for more.

Wander off the main roads now and then. California is fashionable — and often costly — but Washington State has fine attractions, and Oregon Pinot Noir is among the best in the world. Australia is trendy, but there's *so* much variety. Hungary, Yugoslavia, and Spain are not quite so trendy — and also cheaper.

Do try a truly great bottle once in a while. Get everyone to kick in a twenty and buy a three-figure wine. Treat it right and taste it carefully. Is it worth it? If not, you'll save yourself money and envy in the future. And at least you can say, unlike most people, you actually *have* tasted a 1970 Haut Brion or a '79 Château Ausone or a powerhouse vintage Porto and no, it wasn't to your liking.

Put your wine experience into perspective. Value-for-money is probably the best perspective there is. Everyone has tasted Chianti, since those early days of the wicker-covered bottles. But Chianti comes in all shapes and tastes and prices, from squat little bottles to long-necked conversation pieces, from $6 to $60. Some of it can peel paint. Some goes down wonderfully.

And whatever you do, do not pass up domestic wines. It surprises me that so many people still buy the label rather than the wine. They often haven't a clue about vintages or shippers, but if it's old and has a castle on the label they figure it has to be good.

"Oh, local plonk!" said a dinner companion the other night when I put a bottle of B.C. estate wine on the table — a wine that was superior to most of the French blends he'd tasted all year. Your loss, I thought as I sipped a medal-winning varietal white from the Okanagan Valley. Despite what you may still read, there *is* a great deal of very good — and good-value — Canadian wine. Try some and make up your own mind.

Books? Of course, but the choice is endless. It's better to go to the library before you hit the bookstore; check out a few to see if they mean anything — that is, if they address the questions you want answered.

And don't be afraid to ask. There are no dumb questions about wine. If you don't get the answer, ask someone else. And sip a different wine in the meantime. When you run out of things to taste, let me know. We'll start on the Russians, the Romanians, the Argentinians . . .

A Truly Serious Wine Snob's Guide to Rare Wines

———————❦———————

*T*HE RECENT RASH of renewed interest in wines and oenous subjects generated in this country by wine-and-food publications, unscrupulous wine writers like the author, and brash marketeers ready to foist sparkling bilberry wines from Bechuanaland and other exotics upon us, has made for a spate of articles and broadcasts, telling all and sundry what to drink, and how. This has left the Serious Wine Snob without anything on which to lavish serious snobbery. This matter must be remedied.

Cab drivers now readily engage us in conversation, captive-held as we are in traffic jams and late for planes, on the subtleties of the Bordeaux harvest last year, on the case of nouveau they have lying in the trunk, on the many methods of cork removal, on the forty-gallon pail of wine entirely made from eggplant they've got bubbling under the stairs and how it tastes just like real grapes.

Restaurants that heretofore served perfectly acceptable steak and chips with a Labatt's nice and cold on the side have gone ahead with renovations and sommeliers. It's to the point where in most pizzerias you can't get anything to drink that doesn't come with a cork. In my favorite deli they have the wine chilling right next to the stainless-steel bowl of chopped liver. And that's only the red. The white is strung out across the top of the bagel counter in endless variety: medium Riesling, medium Chablis, medium Meursault and my favorite, Ontario Montrachet (medium).

This may all be very nice for ordinary people, but it is easy to see that there is now a void that wants filling, a void created when those selfsame Ordinary People began to discover all the good prestige wines in the world and — worse! — began to actually drink them, and then told their friends.

It has become tremendously difficult to be a proper wine snob, what with coffeeshop waiters curling their lips when you send back the Dinner Red (medium sweet) because there happens to be some sort of large thing floating in the jug standing on your table between the chili and the garlic bread.

It's all well and good to talk about your châteaux, your Lafites and Yquems and Petrus and the like. Everyone is doing that these days. But who do you know, I mean really well, who can claim to have sipped the fabled Château Nougat, the rare almond-flavored table wine of the Ozarks? And while your neighbor may go out and buy the same color Mercedes as the one that's sitting in your driveway, can he claim to have tasted the silken treasure of Clos de Loch Glenmorangie, one of Scotland's most magnificent green wines, aged in a sheep's stomach still within the sheep, and then burned to a crisp over a peat fire?

And who is there among us who truly knows the delights of just one sip of Mardirosian Plinth-Bage, Israel's proudest cremant, with its sprinkling of poppyseed over the inside of the bottle, making it impossible to ascertain the true color of the wine, although it is reputed to be a touch on the blue side?

You see?

In the interests of re-establishing ground for the true, dedicated wine snob, I provide here a guide to some of the world's rarest wines. These are decidedly lesser known, eminently snobbable wines, and the information is presented here for the first time anywhere, doubtless with repercussions to come.

Now that everyone has a pocket edition of Hugh Johnson's in the glove compartment, it is in the interest of all true wine snobs to seek out some of the wines described here. Around the world, numerous wine treasures repose undiscovered, some of them so rare as to never be exported; others are always exported . . . because their producers know something we don't.

Seek them, find them, and as contemporary wine parlance has it, get to first base with them!

❦

ALBANIA: AN EMERGING WINE NATION FLEXES ITS DISUSED VINIFEROUS MUSCLES AND MAKES US WONDER!

One of the most interesting little-known wines comes from this tiny country, shrouded in mystery (both the country and the wine: the country discourages tourism, the wine discourages drinking — the neck of the bottle is encased in cement immediately after bottling). The country is a former friend of China and a more recent football great when the national team took a chunk out of the Celtics, all of which makes for an interesting wine culture. Vineyards there are still called Communist plots; the southern valleys are well suited to corn, wheat, and tobacco, as well as grapes, and there is often some confusion as to which goes into the wine.

The native grape is called rohshoke and is not found elsewhere. A hardy, early-ripening grape, it is thought to have been a successful transplant from China, which no longer wanted anything to do with it. It produces one of the most depressing wines known to man or beast. A drab grey is imparted to the wine by the grape skins. These are actually tiny, woollen coverlets designed to protect individual grapes from frost and which someone forgot to remove prior to the crush.

The seaport town of Durres on the Adriatic is a major Albanian wine region. Just south of Durres, or actually below it, is the famous Likerimat region. The great wine here is the All-Peoples' Riesling Breakfast Wine; it is said, with geographic accuracy, to be produced "under Durres." Also important is the onomatopoeically named town of Puke; the wine produced here is a robust vin du pays generically known as *drivel*, a Gheg word meaning "to walk with the aid of grapefruit." Its price is steep: four goats or, for tourists, surrender of any wide-wale corduroy slacks to the Customs officers.

This is obviously a nation to watch, because as wine prices continue to climb, the discriminating buyer will soon be looking for alternative sources of wine energy. Albania's greatest wine is a hock called Schloss Hoxha; chilling renders it inert long enough to take the cork out. It must then be placed in the garden, and if by sundown it has not yet exploded it could be said to be drinkable. As an accompaniment to Chinese food it is quite good, as an antiseptic perhaps even better. The important thing to remember is to be careful in the handling.

❦

ITALY: LOMBARDY AND PIEDMONT, MOVE OVER — THE NEW KID ON THE BLOCK BRINGS HIS OWN BAT AND BALL!

A little-known Italian wine is Braggadocio Rulente Virulente, a varietal made from the recently cleared aringa grape. Vintages are virtually unknown where this wine is concerned; one was anticipated last Wednesday, but it may have been merely a test of the alarm system.

Where some Italian wines have recently been marketed as "pasta" wines, Braggadocio makes no bones whatsoever about its intent. The little red rooster on the seal is missing, as are some of its teeth. This is a tough wine, and its producers quite rightly position it headfirst, against all comers, as an "anchovy" wine.

Aged for four to sixteen years in industrial-strength plastic, Braggadocio has a unique effluvium all its own. The addition of rock salt in the late stages of tank fermentation makes the wine a bit difficult to enjoy with more subtle dishes but offers the benefit of preserving the wine indefinitely, opened or closed, hot or cold. In a controlled experiment, to commemorate International Geophysical Year, several bottles were lowered to the bottom of the Tyrrhenian Sea, opened, and retrieved several weeks later to reveal the wine still intact. The seaport cities of Livorno, La Spezia, and Massa, however, were closed to shipping for the autumn. The unusual specific gravity of the wine was such that even seawater couldn't get in; you can imagine how it will repel household odors, insects, and other domestic enemies of fine wine.

❦

BORDEAUX: A CENTURIES-OLD TRADITION BUMBLES EVER ON, WITH NOBODY THE WISER!

Château Baron de la Comte de Viscomte Larothe-Fitschild may be the world's most outstanding wine, with a tradition dating back several millennia. It is the only wine to have ever been accorded the highest possible designation under the classification system of 1852 (no longer recognized as the pioneering breakthrough it was). The wine label proclaimed it proudly as being "grand cru classe premier cru supérieur très agréable et convenable pour l'hypermarche." Besides being impressive, it was difficult to get it all typeset on the label.

The château has been in the family of the baron (known to his friends as Le Baron, or in the telephone directory of the tiny town of Puits as Baron, le, M. de, res.) for close to two thousand years, making it the oldest known vineyard in existence. The baron is a charming, forceful, forgetful, and tedious man who often entertains world wine connoisseurs. Indeed, at a recent tasting he produced well over six thousand separate vintages (some of them, admittedly, the midyear vintages introduced by the Citroën company, just shortly after the Mustang). The vineyards of the baron contain all original vine stocks; it is said that his ancestors painted the gates to the vineyards with *confiture d'haricot* (an original family recipe) and the deadly phylloxera passed them by. Less charitable neighbors who didn't get included in the top classification insist that the château's vines were so puny and shrivelled, the phylloxera simply marched on down the road to where they could get a real meal.

When the baron throws open his ancestral cellars to tasters and journalists there is real cause for alarm. At last report, a tasting begun in the spring of 1972 is still in progress, the tasters so far only up to the fall of 1892. Supplies are flown in from time to time. Michael Broadbent is reputed to still be there, and the man who conducts all the wine business around the world under his name is merely a clever, highly paid actor, somewhat disgruntled because he didn't get to go.

The baron made wine history recently when he entrusted all label design to Norman Rockwell. Although dead at the time, the American artist came up with half a dozen fine labels, which adorn some of the bottles today.

Those who have tasted the legendary wine are often struck dumb, sometimes by the clumsy hand of the baron, grabbing the glass back. It has been said to have a taste like "nothing on earth" (*Decanter*), "firmly entrenched in whatever . . ." (*Grape-Nuts: The Magazine of Real Wine Fans*), and "I love that wine, I guess you could say I'm that château-girl" (*Cosmopolitan*).

Saintsbury remembered it as a "golden, glowing, Galapagos kind of wine; I thought it was extinct," while Harry Waugh's *Wine Diary* offers only the enigmatic entry: "19.10.64: Le Baron's latest: hmm, I wonder . . ."

❦

CALIFORNIA: A GOODIE FROM THE GOLDEN BEAR!

Of the thousands of small wineries in the various valleys of California, none can lay claim to producing a product with the down-home punch of Big Mike Dempster's Vintage Table-and-Four-Chairs wine. This is jug wine at its most corrupt. Produced from table scraps and grain alcohol, it nevertheless seems to provide sufficient appeal to have such giants in the field as Gallo taking "a serious look at what this guy is doing!" This may or may not have any direct bearing on Dempster's wine production; possibly it refers instead to his very large collection of rusted cars that surround the winery.

Big Mike Dempster is a former U.S. Marine who got into wine by accident. "I was climbing a fence into somebody's solera terrace," he remembers wistfully, his big hand crushing another tin cup full of his patented sparkling wine, Kickerillo, made through a unique cold-fermentation process and plenty of intimidation. "I knocked over some barrels, they split open, and I slipped into the wine. Before you knew it I was up to my a****jb***nn***s in it!" he says in his colorful colloquial speech rendered virtually incomprehensible by his utter absence of teeth.

The Napa Valley Wine Association, the U.S. Department of the Interior, the CIA, and several environmental associations are working hard to have the winery shut down. Or at least to have some of the cars removed.

The wine itself presents only a slight problem in serving, involving the chipping away of the substance from the side of the glass. Big Mike Dempster insists it isn't a problem if you use Melmac or Styrofoam, both of which make the wine taste better too. The theory that his may be the only winery south of the 49th parallel not owned by Pepsi-Cola is largely conjecture but offers a certain anecdotal value.

❦

BURGUNDY: WINING THROUGH CO-OPERATION!

Le Société Anonyme des Amis de Vin et l'Ail (Capital FF 1,000,000) owns the famous Clos Cloture, which vineyard enjoys the most limited of production. It is reputed to be the smallest vineyard in the world, measuring roughly 6.5 by 8.8 feet (700 fl. oz.; 96 cm³; 104 kilopascals at 15° C; 4:32 p.m., in metric), and is owned by this co-operative of more than four hundred growers, each of whom has several branches. Spirited trading of clusters (cluster-trading or *commerce d'essaim*) goes on well into the night during the spring, and at the Hospices de Beaune auction in mid-November there's not so much talk of casks or bottles as of teaspoonsful (0.05 dL).

The wine can be either white or red, and on occasion even lavender, depending on whether the pickers have washed their hands. Both bottles are numbered each year; there is some friendly rivalry among collectors as to the relative difference in value between #1 (A) or #2 (B).

The Clos also produces a very limited edition nouveau measuring about 6.8 cL (very little, in a cup), a vial of which is flown to London to be enjoyed by the cognoscenti there. At a recent Heublein Rare Wines Auction (the first ever held in Decatur), a vial of the nouveau fetched a record price of $3.80, after spirited bidding between a man who holds a McDonald's franchise on Baffin Island and a masked lady from Gstaad. When it was opened it was discovered to be snakebite serum, erroneously shipped, sparking a giant hunt through the pharmaceutical houses of Europe for the vine with the wine in it, and implicating several shipping firms. The empty vial was turned in several days later at a bottle-refund depot in Hampstead. Many people are still holding their breaths and some, afraid of another wine scandal, are afraid to go out after dark.

The historic château itself has been restored to its former hovel-state and now serves as Le Petit Musée du Vin de Bourgogne (et l'autres directions), a miniature showplace that houses a delightful display of three shovels and a doll said to have been owned by Nicolas Rollins's great-great-great-grandson, Sonny, a musician. La Confrérie des Chevaliers de Pipette et l'Autoclave, a quasi-medical drinking society not in the least related to the

Medical Friends of Wine, gathers there annually for mystic rites and very loud singing. There's been talk in the village of asking them to leave.

❦

GERMANY: THE LAND OF MILCH UND HOCK!
ALWAYS ROOM FOR ONE MORE!

One of this country's truly spectacular precision wines is Siebenzwergenthaler ganz besondere Extratrockenbeeren-aus-lese mit beschrenkter Haftung. This is perhaps the only wine in history that, under Germany's stringent wine laws, received the highest accolade of viticultural quality, the famous Vernünftiger Seal of Ludwig of Bavaria, as a largely meaningless memorial gesture. The Siebenzwergenthaler vineyard is planted with vines at a perpendicular to the sheer cliff face, making harvesting difficult if not downright preposterous. The vineyard workers have revolted against the conditions so frequently that the wine is rarely produced; in this century there have been only two harvests, the 1919 and the 1966. Attempts by the owners to give the vineyard to the union have met with jeers and personal injury, and during both harvests in this century, some six hundred lives were lost attempting to reach the plantings alone. Indeed, the unusual red color of the wine is said to be *"das Blut der Engel oder jemand anderes,"* and other bits of peasant lore abound blatantly.

What makes this such a unique wine is the fact that the grape is left on the vine long after the lese, spätlese, auslese, beeren-auslese, trockenbeerenauslese, and even the infrequent buchl-ese have long taken place. In fact, the grape stays on the vine for another two and a half *years*, until it turns to a white powder. The powder, somewhat resembling the tartar crystals occasionally found in chiefly Mosel wines, has caused more than one import-ing agent to be closely questioned by members of the RCMP.

This powder, after harvesting, is put into the traditional

Zwergenflaschen (oder etwas anderes), flasks in the shape of Bosnia. The wine is obviously dry, as we might expect, but with the addition of some water or a bit of vinaigrette, it makes for a quite delightful taste sensation, perhaps best described by an entertainer who sampled it recently: "Sweet but not too sweet, a little bit lonely, and a whole lotta fun" (Dolly Parton).

❦

JAPAN: THE RISING SUN RISING TO THE CHALLENGE OF A SMALLER, MORE COMPACT WINE WITH BETTER MILEAGE!

This industrial nation is making significant strides in the production of fine wines, and although vineyards aren't plentiful in Japan, there are already two on the northern island of Hokkaido (both owned by Sony) and several more renting space on Mount Fuji. Great advances in computer technology have led the Japanese to produce some stunning wines from materials other than grapes.

Also, the Japanese nomenclature reflects a colorful independence: Ryokan TARBEL is one of the best of the new Japanese transistor wines — light, fruity, quixotic, frivolous, and bouncy, it may well be the only wine in the world that can successfully accompany sashimi.

Another unique Japanese wine derives as a logical extension of the traditional rice-wine brewing technique, resulting in Sake Eiswein. Rice is quick-frozen and then subjected to bombardment by high-speed neutrinos, resulting in a tough, viscous wine that can hold water for up to six days.

Finally, no discussion of the new Japanese wines would be complete without mention of Machigai. This wine, produced from certain rarely benign acids, is frequently drunk after the improper preparation of *fugu*.

CHAMPAGNE: THE RAREST BUBBLES OF THEM ALL!

The great houses of Roederer and Mumm, Krug and Taittinger, blanch at the mere mention of Chilblain. Voltaire, who wrote the famous lines "De ce vin frais l'écume pétillante / De nos français est l'image brillante," refused to discuss Chilblain entirely, unless the aside "As-tu déjeuné, Jaco?" to his landlady can be counted.

This legendary house of Reims came into possession of some four hundred kilometres of underground cellarage by accident and a stupid mistake in the City of Reims public works department. There are those who would have us believe it may have been sabotage. Fortunately, the major houses affected quickly retrieved their bottle stocks before any of the Chilblain family could get to them, but today, the company still manages to produce six or seven bottles of champagne each year, through seepage from limestone adjacencies.

This is the wine of kings, emperors, czars, and regional managers; so good and rare, in fact, that Truman Capote *never* wrote about it at all and apparently Jacqueline Onassis can't even get a soaked-off label to make a lamp with.

Its taste has been described as "silly" and "about what you'd expect" by connoisseurs, and Winston Churchill's reference to the Chilblains' summer mobile home right next to the Pol Roger mansion in Épernay is telling: "One of the most depressing blights on this otherwise majestic street," was how he put it.

Dumas said it should be drunk on bended knee, with the head bared and both arms in a tubful of pudding. "See where that gets you!" he added angrily just before stalking from the room.

The latest successor to the Chilblain fortune, Llewellyn the Taller, works part time as a Council Dullard and freelance consultant to a group of developers who are trying to obtain Reims' first waterslide park. It is apparently to be located on a central site at present occupied by some old church that is far too drafty to be successfully converted into rooms.

CANADA:
THE LAND OF THE MAPLE LEAF IS IN THERE TOO!

Yes, we need take no secondary position to anyone when it comes to producing a fine rare wine, because the Blue Wine of Prince Edward Island (Baby Spud) has been eagerly received by appreciators of wine around town and as far west as Summerside.

It is potassium from the potato-field fallow mixed with the characteristic red soil of the island that produces this distinctive blue wine. An unexpectedly delightful feature is the tendency of the wine, due to its high potassium and magnesium content, to burn under water.

Describing its taste in typical Canadian fashion, wine writer Dan Blank wrote in a recent issue of *Vintages of the Laurentian Shield*, a weekly newsletter: "Sort of, oh, I don't know . . . a bit like . . . well, it's got a kind of definite . . . howyoucallit . . . um, something. But big, oh goodness, yes, big, a big wine. Take the truck when you get that taste happening."

Canadian chronicler of the spoken word John Robert Colombo has taken note of this and is reported to have begun work on *Canadian Quotations About Wine, Volume 1: A to A-Minus*, due next spring from Hurtig of Edmonton.

With all those wines ready for the finding, the serious wine snob need never again be wheedled into ordering yet another tired La Tache or Margaux or Pommery et Greno.

Now you can look the waiter straight in the eye and say: "Bring us six or eight bottles of that Château Malamute '07. Now there's one of the best sparkling wines Alaska ever produced."

And who do you know has even *heard* of that, let alone knocked back a six-pack?

*B*ack to Basics: Handling Wine

————————— ❧ —————————

*N*OW AND AGAIN, it's good to get back to the basics. Where should wine be kept? How long will it keep after it's opened? What's that crumbly white stuff in the bottom of my glass of white wine? These are a few of the basic questions that are often asked. There are basic answers and, sometimes, in the rush to explore new things and sample new tastes, it's easy to forget them.

Then, along comes a handy little checklist, and it makes so much good, basic common sense that it's worth sharing. So pull up a chair, pour a thimbleful of something if the sun's over the yard — or even just the patio — arm, and read along for these few tips on caring for and serving your wine.

First, give it a rest. If you've been on the road, or in the air, for a long trip, *you* need a rest. So does your wine. Whether it's been shipped halfway around the world or cradled on your lap from a secret little Chardonnay boutique in California, let it settle down.

Air travel is particularly tiring for wine. One recommendation is to simply let the bottle rest on its side (like most of us, it can't sleep standing up!) in a dark, cool place for a couple of weeks before opening it.

Why take this lying down? There's a solid reason for storing wines that way, and with the label up. You put the wine on its side just to keep the cork moist. That way, it has less chance of drying out, shrinking, and letting air get at the wine. You can store the wine upside down too (that's the way many wine producers ship their wine, and not just the Australians). Then, a day or so before you want to serve it, bring it back to upright position.

And why should the wine rest with the label up? To disturb its rest as little as possible. You won't have to yard it off the shelf or turn it around to find out what it is before deciding to drink it or put it back. Just slide it gently out of the rack until you can read its name.

Sunlight is good only for the grapes, not for the finished wine, which is why "dark" is part of the cool, dark criteria. Sudden temperature changes won't do it any good either; if you can, ensure that the room's temperature doesn't exceed 18ºC.

One man's room temperature is another's winter carnival! Reds at room temperature, whites chilled. Rule of thumb, with a few exceptions perhaps, and there's always room for experimentation. But here's the key: room temperature doesn't mean hot and chilled doesn't mean iced.

Most red wines taste best at warm room temperature; most whites want only light chilling. Overchilling wallops the stuffing right out of the bouquet and hides the flavors of the wine. Most restaurants serve their white wines far too cold. Try a little experiment. Taste your favorite wine — one you drink often and know well — at three different temperatures: off-the-shelf, chilled for an hour, and iced overnight. You'll be surprised at the marked differences, and you'll find you get more enjoyment from a wine that isn't chattering.

Crystals, diamonds, or just plain crud? How about harmless byproducts of good wine making and a few changes in temperature along the way? Some people are a little alarmed when wine that looks fine and tastes fine is poured into their glass and five minutes later they see a lot of crumbly white bits in the bottom.

Many German wines, and some domestic wines (particularly the Rieslings), tend to precipitate tartrate crystals. These are formed naturally during fermentation and storage. They have no taste of their own and don't influence the taste of the wine. Often, you can anticipate their presence by a bit of crumbly residue on the bottom of the cork the waiter hands you. Pour the rest of the bottle slowly and carefully, sip the wine already in the glass gently, and then ask for a new glass for your refill.

Less is more. Overfilling a wine glass indicates only that your heart — not your eye/hand co-ordination — is in the right place. Don't pour it up to the brim; let there be enough room to swirl the wine without getting it all over yourself or the person beside you. You also want to be able to sniff the aromas that develop in the bulb of the glass, and you can't do that if your nose is submerged.

That's *why they call it stemware!* Hold the wineglass by the stem (brandy snifter by the balloon part, whisky tumbler from the bottom, bottle by the neck, woman by the waist if you're a Bud-man!). (I don't make 'em up, I just listen to the jingles on the country stations!)

There are, again, good reasons. Holding a wineglass by the stem allows you to see the color and clarity of the wine and protects it from the heat of your hand. One more aesthetic — audible — reason. You can make that lovely crystal tinkling sound when you touch glasses with the person across the table from you. Sounds so much more romantic than a dull clunk.

Find a reason to drink it up. Ask someone to help if you have to. Wine exposed to air will experience a change in personality after a day or so. If you haven't finished the bottle you can replace the cork and save it. But in the next day or two it'll become less appealing (unless you have a preserving gadget on hand: vacuum stopper, nitrogen buzzbomb, or one of those expensive French aqualung deals with the hoses).

There are exceptions, as always. The fortified wines are the most notable — sherries, Portos, Madeiras — and also the ultra-sweets — beerenauslesen and Hainle's Okanagan Valley ice wine. (I have to put the plug in here, for these are Tilman Hainle's own thoughtful notes I'm using.) These wines will keep for a week or longer once opened and then carefully stored, without noticeable change in character.

What you've tasted is what you get. Lots of factors influence the way your wine tastes — time of day, food consumed just before, that stick of Freedent you popped in the car, coffee on the run an hour earlier, cigarettes, and the obvious ones like colds and allergies.

Plus perfume. Mostly perfume. And aftershave lotion! Not to mention cologne, hair spray, nail polish, and all the rest. No need to be sexist here either: men are as guilty as women of sending a whole room full of tasters crashing with their designer fragrances. The day Giorgio invents a Zinfandel-based aftershave, we can talk. Till then, how'd you like to wait in the car while we sample this wine?

Food and wine combinations can create palate problems as well: coffee, chocolate, tarragon, vinegar, and, most of all, artichokes. But those you have to find out for yourself, and that's an interesting process of discovery. As you experiment more and more with wine and food combinations, you'll discover not only what doesn't work but also the best part — what does!

Atmosphere counts: good companions, a relaxed, unhurried schedule, a few things to nibble on — the bread should be plain and the cheese too — some neutral water, sparkling or plain to refresh the palate, plenty of serviettes, enough glasses so people can compare one wine with another.

Hey, look what happened: it just turned into a wine-tasting party!

G*rapey, Dusty, Flinty . . .*

—————————❦—————————

MEET GRAPEY, DUSTY, FLINTY, Foxy, Nutty, Woody, Doux, and Brut — eight little wonderwords of wine tasting. There are plenty more, of course, but who can remember them all on a Sunday afternoon? These'll do well enough to dazzle the wine waiter when he brings the Chianti for the lasagna next Friday.

Grapey describes wine that has a pronounced grape taste. The term is generally used pejoratively for wines that are young and immature and haven't yet learned the ropes.

Dusty, on the other hand, is a positive term — except when your car breaks down just the other side of Moosomin — and refers to wine of such great texture that it gives the impression of leaving dust particles of flavor on the tongue. It's not often used to designate Niagara Baco Noir or Okanagan Riesling, but it's a good word for when someone else is picking up the tab but you get to order the wine. Sometimes you can use it at home, when you're changing the bag in the vacuum cleaner and the cat pounces on it.

Flinty refers to a slight — ever so slight — metallic taste present in some dry white wines, especially Chablis. It too is a good thing to encounter. The French take this whole business further still, having coined the term *pierre-à-fusil* (gun flint) for extra-extra dry white wine.

25

Foxy is used for the wild taste of uncultured grapes. Some of them may watch seven, eight hours of TV a day and don't even own a library card. This term often gets thrown at some New York State wines, but any wine can be tarred with the same epithetic brush if it is now, or has ever been, associated with members of the Concord grape family.

Nutty defines spiciness. The reverse is not necessarily true; spicy also defines spiciness, especially in wines like Gewürztraminer. Burgundies and sherries often receive the nutty adjective, as do some Californians. Quite a few of the Californians we saw the other weekend on La Cienega Boulevard with their gold-spiked hair could be recipients of the same appellation.

Woody — Brian Wilson will tell you differently — means a taste of wood in the wine, the result of extended ageing in a cask before bottling. It too is often found in California wines. In that locale, it also refers to a little truck, chopped, channelled, louvred, and covered in six coats of hand-rubbed candy-apple red lacquer. (Oh, *that* Brian Wilson!)

Doux is French for sweet. Sometimes it means very sweet and it is a champagne term. If the wine contains 10 percent or so unfermented sugar by volume, it gets labelled doux, and that puts it decisively in the dessert-wine category. A few drops will do in an emergency on top of your Rice Krispies in the morning.

Brut is at the opposite end of the champagne taste scale. It merely means dry when applied to any sparkling wine. At least, that's what it means everywhere in the world except in a beer parlor in Williams Lake. There, it applies to a heavy-set guy with a green half-ton truck who doesn't like your Lacoste shirt one bit and is coming over to tell you about it!

*S*erving Wine

I CAN REMEMBER MORNINGS when, usually around four o'clock, I would sit bolt upright in bed, reach for my glass of Château de Former Self — too warm by that point, anyway — and fret about how to serve French wine to the party of friends due to arrive in about fifteen hours for dinner and cards.

You'll understand my considerable relief, therefore, at learning from a French publication some time ago that "choosing wines and presenting and serving them requires no special talent, as long as we obey certain essential rules."

Ah, those old certain essentials: one of them always centres on the carrying of a number of high-denomination bills, since French wine of the highest quality tends to send the calculator into error-mode with all the extra numbers.

Another essential deals with how many wines to serve. That's something that has not presented any major worries. It is determined by a number of factors: how close it is to payday; what's in the cellar; who brought some backup bottles to the party. Most of the members of Quincy Memorial Wine Appreciation Circle have long ago learned the answer to the question of how many wines: as many as decently possible and with not too much time in between.

But there is a rule of thumb that suggests, for a simple meal or a snack — a little something to keep the wolf from the camper until you can get to a real meal in the next town — that a single wine is sufficient.

Two might be served: white, then red. For a traditional menu, assert the French, three wines are the magic number. And the sequence is: white with hors d'oeuvres, pâté, or fish; red with the meat and a little to last into the cheese, if you're serving any; then sweet white or semisweet champagne with the pudding.

During prestigious banquets, such as happen around mid-November, when it's Beaujolais time in Burgundy, it is customary to accompany each dish with a different, well-chosen wine.

This is a custom I encourage whenever I can, especially for dinner at someone else's house. The basic sequence is usually chilled sweet (sherry or the like), dry white, dry red, medium red, and sweet white (or maybe port or other fortified, if you feel like lingering a while). But you are allowed to make up your own mind.

Your taste will tell you, after all, what really goes with what, and there's lots of fun to be had in the exploration. So, given that eighteen people are on their way over for chili, the burning question — apart from whether it was the chili powder jar or the paprika shaker you just upended over the pot — is, "How many bottles for how many people?"

The experience of thousands of sommeliers is worth considering: a bottle for two or three people is right, if a single wine is served throughout the meal. If you are serving two wines, one bottle of each may well suffice for four or five people, and when champagne is served to start, provide one bottle for each foursome. If champagne is to accompany the whole meal, make sure there is a bottle for every couple. Of course, this too depends entirely on other factors: Who are these people? What's on the menu? What time is it? Who's picking up the tab?

In Reims, the heart of champagne country, we sat down to a light lunch one autumn day. Lunch was pâté and salmon, chestnut purée and potatoes, a bewildering array of cheeses, and, finally, omelette Sibérienne — baked Alaska over here.

Apart from a lively little red from the local hillsides with the nice name of Bouzy, the wine was champagne throughout, from bone-dry to vintage bubbly worth sonnets, to semisweet to chase the desserts. Amazing how wonderfully champagne goes with just about every food.

Dry young wines don't require any special attention. A couple of hours before serving, you put them in a nice cool room, on the back porch if it isn't midwinter, in the bottom of the fridge, or in a bucket that contains water and ice cubes.

White semisweet wine, sweet wines of most varieties, and champagne should all be cooled longer but still not be served ice-cold.

If the wines are mature — and you can ascertain that by asking any of them if they recall the drum solo out of the Goodman Quartet's recording of "Sing, Sing, Sing" and who played it — bring them from the cellar or from under the stairs the day before and stand them upright in a cool place. Try to avoid shaking the bottle.

Young red wines should come from the cellar an hour or two before the meal and be served cellar-cool.

Gentle handling of wine is essential. When you bring it from wherever it has been stored, keep the bottle horizontal. Gently bring it to an upright position. The idea is to avoid disturbing the deposit of sediment that has formed on the inside of the bottle while it has been resting. Once that has gently settled to the bottom of the bottle, uncork it carefully, give it time to catch its breath, and pour it out gently.

There is an optimum temperature for each variety of wine, and care should be taken to have it reach that temperature *slowly*. I have a friend in Yellowknife who used to put his champagne in a Jolly Jumper and drag it to the Co-op and back behind the snowmobile. It was quick and effective, although it tended to shake the wine up so much it virtually turned to vapor.

Similar experiments with the Château Lunch-Bags under the heat lamp for an hour to get the frost off tended to be less than fully successful. If your red wine is still a touch cool, cup the glass a while with the palms of the hands.

Anyway, it is preferable (says the book) to serve a red wine at a slightly too-low temperature, rather than too warm, since it will warm by three or four degrees in a dining room within ten minutes anyway — whites too, which is why the use of a bucket is recommended.

Finally, these rules to remember:

• The host tastes the wine as soon as the bottle is uncorked. If the wine doesn't come up to expectations it should not be served. This is sensible enough; if you have a bad bottle that you have tasted early enough, there is still time to send out for a replacement or persuade the nice couple in the condo next door to part with some of their stock.

• The wine should always be served before the dish it is to accompany, or at least at the same time. Never after. Some restaurants would do well to have that embroidered on a sampler to hang behind the bar.

• All wines should be served to the right of the guest and with the right hand if you're being at all proper about it — and you're not left-handed. Don't rest the neck of the bottle on the rim of the glass and don't pour the wine from too great a height. Over the guest's shoulder is touchy. Elbow level is nice. Don't fill the glasses to the brim; half is about right if they are big glasses, and a third is better still. ·

And thank goodness someone sat down and figured all this out for us, I say. Now I can go back to sleep.

Greek to Me

———————— ❧ ————————

*T*HE GREEKS HAVE BEEN MAKING wine longer than almost anyone else. They ought to produce better wine than they do — a chilled jar of retsina may help blaze a trail through the roast lamb and onions, but it's hardly the stuff to find in poetry . . . or in Grecian urns. Greece can take the credit for launching European viticulture. Now it has become a matter of the pupils outdistancing the teacher. Neighboring nations generally produce better-quality wines.

Greek wine-making can be traced back some 3,500 years, when the Greeks began planting vines and, being seafarers, sending them around the Mediterranean. Jerez, Malaga, and Sicily owe much of their present successes to those early travellers. The Caspian Sea and Crimea were beneficiaries of Greek viticulture, and there is evidence that, around 600 B.C., the Greeks may have introduced wine growing and production to France. The people of the Rhone Valley haven't looked back since.

Dionysus was the Greek god of wine. His cult attracted happy followers the world over, and he managed to make wine a major item in the balance of trade. Homer sprinkled wine references throughout his *Iliad* and *Odyssey*, plenty of descriptive business about "wine-dark seas" and such. Any decent Greek tragedy

31

counted on wine to get it off the boards, as actors quaffed endless amphorae and accomplished plenty of poisonings.

Before 1500 it was mostly a matter of mead and beer. Later came the vine and the grape. The Minoans learned of wine's delights. From Samos came muscatel. (It still does, and a good one can be a joy!) One wine we find cropping up a lot in Greek Lit was called psithian, a raisin wine that might well have been one of the first trockenbeerenauslesen, those fabulous sweet wines that are made from grapes left to all but dry on the vines, to concentrate the natural sugar into a virtual nectar. My Greek isn't what it used to be, but the statesman Eubulus said it so:

When I'd gathered a thirst
After giving me first
For a sample, and neat
Some psithian sweet.

Well, I don't know what it means either. I think it's one of those fragments off an urn somewhere that gained a greeting-card rhyme scheme and lost a lot of impact in the translation. One Anaxondrides was overheard to mutter, wandering about the Acropolis, "Half a gallon of psithian, mixed . . . , " about which more later.

In those days, Crete was reputed to have made some of the best wines. Alcaeus loved it: "Drink! Why wait for lamps? The day has not another inch to fall. Fetch the biggest beakers, they hang on pegs along the wall." That, you can almost dance to!

Now despite the fact that the Cretans made nice wine, they did the most amazing things to it. Athenaeus remembers, "Wine is sweet when seawater is poured into it." I don't know about you, but the only time that ever got past my palate was at a beach party in Deep Cove back in the sixties, when somebody knocked over the bottle of Faisca that was cooling in the tide. Why seawater in your wine? The ancient Greeks may not only have given us poetry, drama, medicine, and long-distance running, but there's a good possibility they may have given us bartending.

They simply loved mixing stuff with their wine. Seawater was only one thing. Most often, they didn't even bother with a diluted version but just tossed in salt. Pliny made a note that he thought they did this to "enliven the smoothness of their wines." Seawater, pine resin, and even perfume were fair game.

Dexicrates recalls a particular weekend: "And if I tipple, I drink my wine with snow and a dash of the finest scent Egyptians know." Try it at dinner next time you're at the Empress Hotel. Borrow the lady's little purse-flask of Calèche, put a few drops in the glass, and pour in some Black Tower. Just see how fast a friendship can fade!

If you think you're paying a lot for wine these days, consider that in 89 B.C. the Roman censors (forerunners of our liquor boards) fixed the price of Greek wine at four hundred sesterces per amphora. An amphora ran about twenty-six litres, so you paid about fifteen sesterces per litre of wine. I don't know the rate of exchange, but the average day rate for a free (as opposed to enslaved) Roman laborer was three sesterces — so he worked all day Monday through Friday to earn enough for a bender.

Old Greek wines included many things our palates would find odd indeed. Abates was a laxative wine (!), while deuterias was an early light wine made from grape skins soaked in water. Gleucos was sweet, unfermented grape juice, and hepsema a mix of various grapes and sugar, boiled till it became almost syrup.

From the island of Lesbos came protropon, which was made from the must that bled from the grapes before they were pressed. A similar method is still in use in Hungary in the production of Tokaji Essencia. Melitites was made from honey, salt, and raisins, and Oxymel combined honey, salt, vinegar, and rainwater with grapes, all heated to boiling a dozen times before it was ready to drink.

Although there are some quite respectable Greek wines to be

enjoyed when one is cruising the islands or sipping in the shadow of the Acropolis, we get to taste few of them in Canada. Mostly we have what most people know — sum total — about Greek wines: retsina. And a retsina, unless you're Greek or adventuresome, or both, can be a mind-wrenching experience first time out. I've known grown men to crumble at the edges when faced with a glass of what they deep-down know to be antiseptic solution for swabbing the decks of a Great Lakes ore carrier.

The typical first-timer's reaction to retsina is easily ameliorated. The wine must be drunk as cold as possible. Put it in the fridge for a week or so, until it is chilled to the point where it hurts the head if you gulp down half a glass. Forget everything you know about not chilling wine; retsina needs to get as close to freezing as possible.

Furthermore, you don't swirl, sniff, and sip. What you do is put it into a tumbler and set it alongside a platter of chopped onion and yogurt, crispy grilled lamb and roast potatoes, deep-fried squid, sausage — whatever. That's how to drink retsina. Funny thing: after a glass or so, you no longer taste the Pine-Sol and it goes down almost as well as the late Mr. Pibb.

But retsina is only a fraction of what Greek wine is all about. Greece also produces table wines — white and red — sweet wines, and sparkling wines. Total production is a little more wine than Bordeaux puts out: more than 640 million litres a year. A small bit of puzzlesome legislation surrounds the best of it, and while the French and Germans and Italians, with their Denominazione system still barely out of the shrink wrap, would throw up their hands in disbelief, the Greeks aren't bothered a bit.

Happily, they sip dozens of litres per person per year, and they rank twelfth in total world production by volume. The largest amount comes from the Peloponnesian peninsula, and most of it is sweet. From Macedonia, which borders Yugoslavia and Bulgaria, come good reds and whites, and even today wines from Rhodes, Crete, and Samos rank among the best. So do the wines of Patras — the wines of Achaia-Clauss.

There are few spots in the land of the Hellenes as beautiful as the place where Gustav Clauss established the Achaia-Clauss Wine Company. High on a hill in the Panahatkon Mountains, the winery and vineyards cover sixty hectares, commanding a magnificent view. The town of Patras is nearby, and thousands of visitors come to see and sample every year.

Gustav Clauss came here from his native Bavaria in 1845 to work with a trading company. Fond of the outdoors, he built a hut as his retreat in the hills. Later he bought a few hectares of vineyard and started making wine for his own pleasure. Friends found the quality so outstanding they offered plenty of encouragement, and in 1861 Clauss founded the company that still bears his name. He used the most scientific methods then known in the production of his wines and later began to purchase other vineyards in the area.

Today, Achaia-Clauss is still a family business, the Antonopoulos family having purchased the operation from the Clauss estate. In any given year, the company produces more than 10 million gallons of wine and spirits, of which almost three-quarters stays at home. The rest goes around the world, to the delight and acclaim of millions of appreciative fans. Achaia-Clauss is the largest wine company in Greece, and its list of products runs to more than thirty items. Among them are the following that can be found in Canada.

Santa Helena white wine: dry, crisp, and refreshing, it benefits from a little breathing after chilling and rewards the palate with a clean, honest flavor.

Castels Danielis red wine always carries a date, and its history goes back to 820 A.D. It is light and lively, akin to Beaujolais, and good value.

Demestica white and red are usually served as everyday table wines. The white is very light and dry with good fruit, making it ideal for summertime sipping. The red is similar to Valpolicella — light and slightly springy and wanting a chill on it to make a fine after-tennis cooler; it's terrific at lunch. (Both are frequently misspelled as Domestica, but they do in fact take their name from the mountain village of Demestica.)

Château Clauss red is a vintage-dated, well-aged wine with good color, plenty of depth and body, and a resounding fullness. It wants room temperature and an hour to breathe; then it rewards with a pleasant flavor still retaining a slight tannin edge and already starting to carry a coppery tinge. Soft and sippable, it's consistent in quality.

Mavrodaphne is the unique sweet wine of Greece and, more particularly, of Achaia-Clauss, being the company's own appellation contrôlée. The wine was created by Gustav Clauss in tribute to the woman he loved. He took the mavroudi grape as the wine's principal component and then added her name — Daphne — to achieve a sweet, rich, satisfying dessert wine that comes off as a cross between port and sherry with a dash of Madeira thrown in. It's nutty and round and ruby.

Ouzo is 45 percent alcohol, so watch out. The producers call it a dry aperitif and the anise-flavored classic is common to all Mediterranean regions. Clear in the bottle, it becomes opalescent when mixed with water. The licorice taste is soft enough, but ouzo packs more punch than brandy.

Speaking of which, brandy from Greece is unmistakable. Although there are different types and strengths and ageings, most of it has a characteristic flowery bouquet and softly perfumed yet pungent flavor. It's perfect with Greek coffee and baklava for dessert. Some places insist on serving it in a snifter, which is silly, since that tends to concentrate the heady aroma and direct it up your nose, making you cough. It is best in a liqueur or shot glass.

These wines (and spirits) are the ideal accompaniment to the Greek cuisine that is now much in evidence in Canada.

Maybe this summer is the time to do one of those lamb barbecues. And if your only previous experience with Greek wines has been with retsina, give yourself a taste of some of the others. Maybe you'll end up wanting to engrave some poetry on the side of a sugar bowl.

*S*pain and Portugal for Starters

❧

*M*OST OF US CANADIANS tend to think little — and know less — about the table wines of Spain and Portugal. To be sure, they creep into the proceedings occasionally; from Spain, Yago's red and white in the distinctive long-necked bottles have made many friends, not just because of their very reasonable cost, and some of Portugal's rosés, notably Mateus, are bestsellers. But that's about it.

Yet both countries produce a considerable variety of table wines. And though truly excellent Spanish and Portuguese wines may seem rare, they do exist. Some can rival first-rate French wines.

Spain boasts more land under vine cultivation than any other country in the world. Yet its wine production measures only one-third that of Italy's. There are several reasons.

To start with, a Spanish vineyard may often contain other crops — olive trees and patches of wheat, for instance — interspersed with the vines. Also, rainfall in the southern and central areas isn't plentiful, resulting in exceptionally arid soil. Perhaps the main reason is difference in attitude: with the exception of Jerez (which in any case produces sherry, not table wines) and to a lesser extent Rioja, most Spanish wine regions are fairly casual about geographic definition and production methods and values.

Spain's three major wine regions are, respectively, in the north, along the Mediterranean shores, and on the central plateau. In the north (which includes Galicia, the Basque provinces, and Oviedo) the Rioja district produces what many believe to be the country's finest table wines. The name Rioja applies to a stretch of land about 130 kilometres long in the valley of the Ebro River, although it's actually derived from an Ebro tributary, the Rio Oja. Here, sloping vineyards along the riverbank constitute a charming and attractive wine landscape.

The Mediterranean wine-producing regions are Catalonia, where Barcelona and Tarragona are among the major centres, and Andalusia, whose main centres are Cádiz, Granada, Málaga, and Seville.

The largest region is that of the central provinces, probably best known for its Valdepeñas wines. The name, which means vale of stones, applies to a growing region that is similar to that part of the Rhone Valley that produces Châteauneuf-du-Pape. Valdepeñas produces both reds and whites; the former are often regarded as being the better, and some of them are certainly quite fine.

In fact, red wines are Spain's forte in general; the country's climate is not conducive to great white wine production. For all that, Rioja has borrowed the names Chablis and Sauternes and produces respectively dry and sweet white wines under those names. Another Spanish white quite commonly seen in Canada is the sparkling Codorniu, which has eased the price of popping champagne corks at countless weddings and parties across the country.

But for the really fine quality in Spanish wines, look to the red reservas of Rioja. They're often ten, twelve, or even fifteen years of age, and in spite of recent inflation-induced price increases, they may well be the best value for money of any red wines available today. They certainly do not compare unfavorably with some still higher-priced Burgundies and Bordeaux.

Reading a Spanish wine label is in general far less complicated than reading a German or French one. "Denominacion de

Origen," a statement similar to France's appellation contrôlée, guarantees the origin of the product, while "reserva" indicates a high-quality wine that the shipper has selected for additional maturing in cask or bottle.

Some of Rioja's reservas — among them the Duque de Sevilla wines recently introduced into Canada — are aged by a process borrowed from Spain's sherry producers. This is the solera system. A solera is a group of barrels of various ages. The oldest among them may even have been made from oak brought to Spain from the Western Hemisphere by the Spanish conquistadores more than four centuries ago. Wine drawn off for bottling always comes from the oldest cask. That cask is then refilled with wine from the second-oldest barrel, and so on down the line. Hence, new wine is always added to the solera at one end as old wine is taken out at the other.

Only Spain's finest wines are produced in this painstaking way, and the government agency, the Consejo Regulador Denominacion de Origen, guarantees that at least 75 percent of the contents of each bottle is of the vintage specified on the label. This is a notable exception to the situation prevalent in other Spanish wines, where a date may often be so much window dressing.

(There's an interesting sidelight to the Duque de Sevilla operation, which is in the Cariñena area of the province of Aragon. Many years ago, Spanish monks transported cuttings from the area, particulary from the duque's vineyards, to California. These were planted and today grow in great abundance as California's Carignane grapes, the basis of many fine California wines.)

Lesser Spanish table wines are quite agreeable, although, unlike the reservas, they seldom age well in the bottle. But what they may lack in character and greatness, they usually make up in price.

And it's always worth keeping a wary eye open. Some years ago, in a liquor store on Edmonton's south side, I found a single bottle of a Rioja red called Lopez de Heredia Tondonia, 1954 vintage, lying on a shelf. No one seemed to know much about it, and the $4.40 price tag was reasonable enough for experimentation. It was perhaps the greatest Spanish wine I've ever tasted. It possessed an excellent character, full body, and delightfully heady bouquet. Its age was evident from a slight mustiness, which didn't detract once the wine was allowed to breathe. It had a very full ruby color. In all, it was a clean, robust, and fine wine that called for more. Unfortunately, there wasn't any more. But as more and more specialty stores and specialty shops open across Canada, I keep on looking . . .

André Simon, the famous oenophile, described Portugal as "the most wine-conscious country in the world." That may well be; the average annual per-capita consumption is 125 bottles of the stuff.

Portugal's wines can be divided into two prime groupings: vin ordinaire and quality wine. Vin ordinaire is just that, ordinary table wine in all its possible permutations. But they approach some of the appellation contrôlée products of France, both in flavor and bouquet and in the guarantees of origin the names offer.

To date, controls have been established for six categories of Portuguese wine — Vinho Verde, Dão, Bucelas, Colares, Carcavelos, and Setubal.

Vinho Verde literally means green wine. In fact, it may be either a red or a white. The reference is not to the color but to the wine's youth and instability. Light-bodied, low in alcohol, and often mildly sparkling, it comes from northern Portugal. Most Vinho Verde is drunk locally; wines chosen for export are likely to be mellow rather than crisp, not unlike a mild white Bordeaux.

Dão wines — red, white, and rosé — come from central Portugal. They are vinhos maduros, which means they have been allowed to age a year or two longer than vinhos verdes. Hence, they have more fruit and body and, because of careful blending, are better balanced. Long popular in Portugal, they have more recently made deserved inroads in Canada.

Bucelas wines are named for a village about twenty-five kilometres north of Lisbon. They are fair-quality whites, which, however, are not often seen in this country.

Colares is a region remarkable for two reasons. Its vines are rooted in sand dunes along the Atlantic coast. And they are of a variety that proved immune to phylloxera, the dreaded vine-killing insect that destroyed so many European vineyards about a century ago. Production is small, so we don't often see its acceptable reds here; they're well worth searching out if you're travelling in Portugal.

Any discussion of Carcavelos and Setubal — and of Madeira, famous product of Portugal's offshore island of that name — takes us into another realm, for these are sweet wines, usually drunk as the finish to a meal, as is port, the country's most celebrated product of the vine.

In the world of wine, however, nothing is graven in stone, as I discovered in Lisbon a couple of years ago.

Having been lured by the *Guide Michelin*'s one-star rating for the Restaurant Michel (one of the country's very few Michelin-starred restaurants), we engaged a crusty old diesel-powered Mercedes taxi to take us to the place. It was a long drive, through narrow streets, high up alongside the castle walls on the hill overlooking Lisbon. The cab's already scarred fenders threatened to tear laundry from lines and scrape the sides of ancient buildings, and there was much dodging of chickens and children.

Once at Michel's, there was an even more unsettling experience. This was the suggestion of the restaurant's operator that we should, with our meat course, drink the bottle of 1945 port that I had managed to obtain in Oporto a day or two earlier and with which I had planned to end the meal. But to everyone's surprise it worked. What we had thought would be an uncommonly sweet accompaniment to a main course made for an unusual but most complementary blend. Dinner ran on into the small hours. Finally we drove back down the hill through the old town, listening to Blood, Sweat and Tears on the cab radio and reflecting once again that the Iberian peninsula often produces delightful surprises — particularly when it comes to good food and good wine.

Marsala, Sweet Marsala

ONE OF THE SWEETEST wines of them all comes from Sicily. The fabled Island in the Med, just an easy kick off Italy's big toe, comprises the second-biggest wine region in that country. That's mainly because of the Marsala, a delicious sweet, rich wine that makes its way from there to appreciative palates and wonderful desserts around the world.

Marsala is a fortified wine, of the same ilk as port, sherry, Madeira, and Malaga. Its alcohol content runs 18 to 20 percent — as opposed to table wine's more genteel 10 to 14 percent. It is the English who were ultimately responsible for making it a hit, just as they did with port and sherry and Madeira.

Unlike many other wines, Marsala has both a definite place of origin and a recorded birth date.

It was 1773 when the wine was, for all intents and purposes, invented by one John Woodhouse of Liverpool. While Sicilians were producing the wine from local grapes for their own enjoyment, it was the Englishman who recognized it at once as a worthy competitor to other sweet fortified wines — wines the English were consuming by the hogsheads and pipes and barrels and bottles.

Woodhouse also wasn't blind to the fortuitous fact that the higher alcohol content would keep the wine from spoiling on the long sea voyage from Sicily to Britain. So he set about organizing its export and arranging for its shipment.

Marsala is made from two Sicilian grapes, the catarato and the grillo, with just a smidgen of inzolia added for good measure. A mix of 25 percent passito (dry grape must) is added, along with unfermented fresh grape juice. Then it's all boiled down to a suitable thickness. The process causes additional fermentation to take place. It also gives the wine its dark brown-red color.

Most Marsala is made in this manner, although some is produced by the solera method — just like sherry — which requires a continuous blending of older wines with new wines so, ultimately, every bottle contains at least a minuscule amount of very ancient wine.

Marsala comes in different grapes: fini, superiori, vergini and speciali. Fini has the lowest alcohol content — 17 percent — and is usually kept for cooking. Superiori requires at least two years' ageing and is sometimes called Garibaldi or cooli (hill wine). Vergini is the finest quality Marsala, always produced by the solera method and allowing very few, if any, additives.

Additives, though, are the name of the game for speciali, the flavored Marsalas. Included in this category are Marsala all'uovo, as well as Mandoria, Fragola, and even Caffè, which was briefly available in Canada. These Marsalas, known as the creams, have almond, orange, strawberry, fruit syrups, and, most often, eggs added to them. That makes them very sweet, thick, and syrupy, if lacking the finesse of flavor of the other varieties.

Marsala is probably most familiar as the all-important ingredient in a good zabaglione, the feather-light dessert I've never been able to master. Somehow, scrambled eggs with Marsala, which is the way mine has always turned out, isn't quite right after veal scaloppine — or anything else for that matter!

In a small sipping glass, though, the wine makes a pleasant alternative to sherry, and, like sherry, it can be enjoyed at the beginning of a meal as well as at its conclusion. So good an alternative to sherry was it for Admiral Nelson that he embarked on one return voyage to Britain with 160,000 litres of it in the hold.

Marsala made John Woodhouse a rich man. Soon, other Englishmen came along to establish new techniques of cultivation, production standards, and a distribution network all catering to an eager market.

In the past few years, Canadians have come to relegate it to the back of the shelf, which is unfortunate, since the taste is delicious: a little like old sherry, combining some of the "caramel" of Madeira with its own special qualities. "A toasted wine with a scent like beef broth," says Hugh Johnson, who finds it superior to sherry by far as an addition to consommé and other clear broths.

They say the name of the wine comes from the Arabic *marsh-el-allah* or harbor of Allah. How to enjoy it, apart from with soups and in desserts?

As a dry aperitif, chilled. As a companion to strong cheese as well as fruit, not quite so cool. Use it to flavor veal scallops, of course, but also mushrooms, game, and risottos of any kind. As a sipping wine it has been enjoyed for years, earning the label of *vino da meditazione* along the way. It's also fine for baking.

Whether you enjoy it with food or in it, in a tiny glass or a long drink, here's to John Woodhouse for getting it started on its way to us more than two centuries ago — and to Sicily for keeping it coming.

The Eiswein Cometh

———————— ❧ ————————

WHEN DINNER'S BEEN A SUCCESS and at long last talk turns to Bordeaux vintages and crusty port, throw this one into the ring: eiswein. It's pronounced pretty much the way you'd think — "ice-vine." It isn't something Anne Murray might have sung about, nor is it a cheeky name for what's left in the glass after the rocks have melted.

Eiswein is one of those German (it had to be!) numbers that only comes about under a certain set of conditions. It's rare, rich, wonderful, and costs a bundle. Sometimes you see it in the rare-wines stores, more often you have to bring it back from overseas. Explaining it to the folks at Customs is, shall we be euphemistic and say, difficult. But you might easily become a confirmed fan, provided your taste in wine runs to the rich, flowery, full, sweet-but-never-cloying German style of white.

Eiswein is made from grapes that have been left on the vines so late into autumn that it's become winter. Sooner or later there's a frost, and then if the grower has some good grapes left, he can get busy and produce an eiswein. The customary practice is to harvest the grapes before dawn, because they must reach the crusher and be pressed before they thaw. In some years, eiswein is produced as late as January (which means that the wine becomes the earliest to bear the new year's vintage).

45

Some people dismiss eiswein as a mere curiosity, although it's generally accepted that only the better producers become involved in it. For one thing, it's a considerable gamble: if the grapes are good and the wine makers are paying top marks, there's no small temptation to get the harvest over and done with, rather than carefully select better bunches of grapes and leave them hanging on the vines in hopes of a good early frost.

Eiswein is elegant and rich, although it doesn't quite come up to the burst of intensity in taste produced by beerenauslese or trockenbeerenauslese (more on these in a bit). It's an after-dinner wine or an extra-dinner wine; hardly the sort of thing you serve when the "choice is red or white," and for the producers hardly a commercial proposition. But the German wine makers and growers are proud of these oddities; Hugh Johnson hits the nail squarely when he tells us that of course eiswein has to be a German proposition, for "the German wine growers love showing off."

There isn't quite the mystique surrounding eiswein now that there once was. Years ago, eiswein made on specific holidays took the name of that day. Consequently, if it was made on the sixth of December it was St. Nikolaus Eiswein; if it happened on Christmas Eve it was Christabend of Weihnachtseiswein, and so on. There were nice old names from saints galore for wines made on virtually any day in December and beyond. But the new, efficient, tighter-than-tight German wine laws have altered all that: now there's just plain eiswein, and there you are.

Unlike trockenbeerenauslese wines (TBAs), eisweins can't be kept too long. Reasonable age won't harm them for the most part, but very old eisweins are rare; the cost of laying them down is prohibitive. (My few bottles of '59 Thiergarten are still in the cellar; I can't offer you any personal tasting notes except for a reflection on the little I sampled on the Moselle in 1973: it was then absolutely stunning, rich and velvety, quite unlike any wine I'd ever tasted.)

Eiswein is a special category in German wine, and that must

be indicated on the label, where the designation appears after the designation of quality (Auslese Eiswein, for example).

It needs good grapes, a good growing season, and then frost. There's generally plenty of opportunity for that, since most of Germany's vineyards are in the same latitude as Newfoundland. Because of the country's fairly difficult, cool climate, the German wine harvest is delayed as long as possible anyway, with usually not much happening before October. By then enough sun has come along to make for a good balance of sugar and acid. (German growers contend that 100 days of sun between May and October is what's required for a good wine; 120 will produce great wine.)

A quick primer in how the 1971 German wine laws go: Tafelwein is the plonk (der Plonk!); QbA comes next (and nobody ever tells you what that stands for: *Qualitätswein mit bestimmter Anbaugebiete* or wine from a particular region and designated grape variety — as in Liebfraumilch), and then QmP or *Qualitätswein mit Prädikat*, that elusive term that means something like class or breeding. QmPs are the best of the lot, and are always kabinett (the first harvesting and the driest wines), spätlese (late harvest), auslese (late harvest, specially selected), beerenauslese (individually picked grapes, chosen for ripeness and uniformity), and then TBA (grapes that have been attacked by the old botrytis — that beneficial mold that shrivels the grapes skins and concentrates all the sugar inside — and chosen for their high degree of natural sugar).

I once asked an associate, who'd spent a few years working in the wine business on the Moselle and Rhine, precisely when the Germans would drink eiswein. As writer Alec Waugh stated, German gastronomy is built around beer, but they do drink wine and lots of it, the best before dinner or after and at special social occasions. My friend said that the luxurious eisweins were often uncorked at midnight on New Year's Eve and similar portentous events.

I remember a Josef Milz 1973 Binger St. Rochuskapelle Auslese Eiswein. I drank it one afternoon sitting in one of those picture postcard castle ruins, watching the barges heading down the Mosel River. It was as fine an occasion for eiswein as any I remember!

Since it is an exception, not a regularly obtainable kind of wine, you have to keep your eyes and ears (not to mention line of credit) open for some. There was eiswein in 1961 and 1973. Doubtless, there are some producers who go for it every year. But it is a tricky and colorful harvest. Elaborate alarms are set in the vineyards, rigged to thermometers with bells and buzzers that sound in homes down the hillside. When the mercury drops, the alarms go off, fires get lit, flashlights and torches illuminate little processions of grumbling pickers who've been wakened out of warm feather beds to tromp around the vineyards in the middle of the night. Then there's lots of eminently fortified coffee and little flasks of trester, the Moselle's version of the super-distilled marc, a little of which will cause the blood to course through the body long enough to get the grapes to the crusher, and a little more of which can put you into a comatose condition! The slopes are noisy with harvesters, and tiny villages have carts clattering along the cobbles and tractors grunting through the night and crows shrieking in the trees and dogs dancing and the occasional cat creeping along a balustrade highly perplexed by it all. And so it even makes the best of us turn to purple prose!

There was a 1980 eiswein. I recall a telex from the St. Ursula Weingut at the Scharlachberg vineyard of the Villa Sachsen at Bingen on the Rhine. Apparently, 1980 marked the first time in two hundred years that the grapes for eiswein of this estate were picked in January. The '80 eiswein Riesling auslese and beerenauslese were picked on the weekend of the twelfth and thirteenth of January, with outside temperatures of -7 and -10°C respectively. That made it the first 1980 wine crop in the Northern Hemisphere.

Prices for the admittedly exquisite oddity are always ridiculous. Years ago, an eiswein we drank in California sold at U.S. $27 the half-bottle. I've paid as much as $60 for a bottle, and that too was a decade ago. A minimum for an eiswein in Canadian stores would be in the vicinity of $40 to $60, especially with provincial markups.

Is it worth it? By all means. Although not nearly as room-filling in its bouquet or as dazzlingly heady in taste as a well-vintaged TBA, there's a quality to eiswein that is entirely distinctive. The experience, not to mention the tradition and histories (and histrionics!) behind it, are all worth the cost. If your dealer or liquor board offers you one, or if you see some at Sherry-Lehman in New York, pick up a bottle. If you're disappointed, send me what's left in a Thermos!

Calvados: Small Consolations for the Coffee

———— ❦ ————

*T*HERE WAS A TIME, not all that many years ago, when brandy after dinner was the standard state of affairs. But over the past decade or so I've drifted away from the noble Courvoisier and turned my after-dinner attentions to such delights as the clear, fresh eaux-de-vie of pear and raspberry and plum and the particular pleasures of Calvados. (Well, every once in a while I'll succumb to the still-noteworthy charms of Louis Treize — particularly when travelling in the Orient, and always when someone else is buying!)

Calvados is a brandy whose principal ingredient is apples rather than grapes. So at its most basic it's apple brandy. There are two primary sources of the stuff: the United States (where it's commonly called applejack), and France, where the best known is Calvados, named after the department in Normandy, which is the country's centre of apple and cider production. Considerable amounts are also made in Brittany. The production of Calvados begins with the juice of ripe, healthy apples being left to ferment for a month or more until all the sugar is out; then the liquid is distilled. Calvados pays d'Auge is the crème de la pomme, and like fine whisky it is distilled only in pot stills. (Ordinary French apple brandy of no particular appellation is called eau-de-vie de cidre.)

The pays d'Auge is a double-distilled Calvados, making its production similar to cognac's. The color comes from the oak barrels in which the Calvados is aged, and ageing can take as long as forty years, if not more.

The people who are behind the most recent marketing push for Calvados are called the BNICE, which stands for Bureau National Interprofessionnel des Calvados et Eaux-de-vie de Cidre et de Poire. (It's not something you'd want to have to answer the phone with every time it rings! "Bee-nice" would make a handy and mellifluous acronym.) Its duties are to supervise the production of Calvados and apple brandy: stocking, ageing, and promotion on international markets.

Although there aren't any formal documents that deal with the origin of Calvados, its history has been common knowledge in Normandy for at least four hundred years. The actual "inventor" is thought to have been the Sire of Gouberville, an agronomist with a taste for the better things in life who lived in the sixteenth century on the Channel coast, at Mesnil-au-Val. Why nobody else had ever thought of distilling the juice of all those nice apples from around there isn't known, but it's a good thing somebody finally got around to it.

There's no mistaking it from the first sniff or sip: a pronounced apple aroma and flavor are very much in evidence in this attractive amber liquid. It was Calvados that contributed significantly to the impressive reputation that Normandy has acquired over the centuries, as a place where fine food is the order of the day — any day. Here, people often drink it in the straight-back-in-the-middle-of-the-meal-to-make-room-for-more manner, known as *trou normand*. (One bit of promotional literature I came across not long ago put it this way: "For example, after the tripe and before the leg of lamb or the roast duck . . .")

But it's fine after a meal, too: in fact, there's a little tradition associated with it called consoling the coffee. You sip a nice strong after-dinner cup, and then while the cup's still warm, pour in the Calvados and let it mingle with the remaining few drops.

Calvados is absolutely essential for cooking, and you'd be surprised what a vast variety of dishes benefit wonderfully from a tablespoon or two of the noble apple brandy. Pâté is a natural, as are chicken breasts, veal, tripe, (of course, since that's one of the regional specialties), apple desserts, crêpes, and various pastries.

Those all seem fairly standard, but how about filets of sole prepared with white wine, cider, and Calvados, green grapes, cream, and butter? Or homards à la Normande: cayenne, shallots, Calvados, cream, parsley, and other surprises?

There are hundreds more; in fact, any good French cookbook will probably spell them out. As far as the ongoing enjoyment of Calvados in our part of the world is concerned, therein lies a small problem: it has to do with money, of course.

So the next time you've got dinner guests over and you're starting to set out the liqueurs, add another dimension to after-dinner enjoyment: bring out a bottle of apple brandy and get set to console your coffee.

Something to Shout About: Screech

———————————❧———————————

MY FIRST EXPERIENCE with this uniquely Canadian spirit came as a result of one of those six-ounce shirt-pocket mickeys a slightly incredulous acquaintance from Europe had picked up at a refuelling stop in Gander, Newfoundland, on his way west.

"Here," he said, handing me the little bottle as though it could explode in his hands any second. He handed the lady of the house a bouquet of flowers with much more practised aplomb. He was visiting for dinner.

"Um, don't bother to open it on my account. Put it in the — " he hesitated, just a fraction too long to be fully credible "cellar. Let it rest . . . or whatever it's supposed to do."

The gentleman's perplexity was understandable. There he was, scion of one of those old, established European wine-houses, first-time-visitor-to-our-maple-leaf-encrusted-shores types, and his first encounter with something that had alcohol in it was labelled Screech. It's a wonder he stayed for dinner.

From that moment, I, however, was hooked; the name alone assured that. Anything called Screech, proud and plain, had to be something to keep in the house for special occasions. For months, I lived off the vicarious kick of the label alone. Then one night it was sampled. Quickly back to the thrills of the label!

No, it really wasn't as head-blowing-off as the name might

imply. If you have ever sampled Screech, you might thereafter ask them at the liquor store to discreetly slip it into a plain brown bag.

Screech is rum. "Premium quality, dark Jamaican, bottled and aged in Newfoundland," according to the legend on the label.

But why the name? "Long before liquor boards were created," reads the little pamphlet from its national distribution agency, "the Jamaican rum called Screech was a mainstay of the Newfoundland diet." Apparently, the island shipped salted fish to the West Indies and got rum in return. "The fish became a national dish in Jamaica, and the rum a traditional drink of Newfoundlanders."

In those days, rum was high in alcohol and not so swift as far as taste went. When the government took over the Newfoundland liquor business in the early part of this century, it packaged the rum in a sophisticated-looking, but unlabelled bottle. Luckily for all concerned, they left the stuff inside alone. And so this delightful little potion could have continued on its merry way forever as a nameless local rum, except for the influx of our Canadian servicemen to the island during the Second World War.

The story goes that a commanding officer of the first detachment to arrive was taking advantage of Newfoundland hospitality. He was offered a drop of the hard stuff as an after-dinner drink. Watching his host toss it back without hesitation, our unsuspecting mainlander followed suit and downed it in one. The poor chap let out a howl of protest as soon as he got his breath back . . . sometime later that evening.

Sympathetic neighbors rushed to the house to help the poor creature that sounded like it was in such agony. Among the first to arrive was an old sergeant who pounded on the door and shouted, "What was that ungodly screech?" The laconic Newfoundlander who came to the door replied, "The Screech? 'Tis the rum, son."

A legend was born.

Word got out, and the soldiers were determined to sample it

for themselves. They found its effects quite as devastating as the name implied. It became a favorite for all that, and soon the Newfoundland Liquor Board, with considerable marketing panache, labelled it The Famous Newfoundland Screech.

Apparently it is still the most popular alcoholic drink consumed there, but its growth market now covers the country and may be threatening the palates of unsuspecting Europeans. Screech is no longer the dregs of the kegs; quality and consistency are subject to constant analysis, and the Jamaican origin assures its special character. It's quite a nice rum, although its proof strength has been knocked down to 70 from the original 100. Still, there's a kick to it, and though it's unlikely you'll howl after your first sip, I would keep an eye on my coat and a hand on my wallet after three or four.

Some things you may want to know if you're not quite prepared to toss it back Newfoundland-style: A Newfie Bullet consists of an ounce each of Screech and coffee liqueur, blended over chipped ice. A Muffled Screech is an ounce of the stuff, a quarter ounce of Grand Marnier, and a couple of ounces of cream. Come-by-Chance calls for an ounce of Screech, a quarter ounce of Grand Marnier, four to six of fresh orange juice, and a little something on top to make it look nice. Island Bliss is Screech and pineapple juice, milk, and coconut syrup. Of course, you can flame it, parfait it, and do a Newfie Coffee with it.

Now, then, what can we do with all those extra grapes in the Okanagan that might have a similar effect? Well, first we have to create a little legend . . .

A *Chequered Past: Gin*

———————————— ❧ ————————————

MOTHER'S RUIN WAS one of the nicer terms. Many called it a lot worse names. Hogarth etched some memorable scenes about it. William of Orange and Queen Anne helped its industry along. At least four geographic locales claim to have invented the most famous cocktail based on it. During Prohibition it moved into the bathtub and the speakeasy. Earlier, it was sold for a penny a glass in not very palatial "palaces." People take it neat, iced, mixed, pink, salty, sweet, fizzed, and stirred, not shaken. It goes into more cocktails than any other liquor. Most of us got drunk on it at least once, usually in high school. It happened to me in the parking lot of a motel in Medicine Hat, and it was a decade before I could get next to a bottle of it again.

Gin. Three little letters identifying a colorless, subtle-tasting, innocent-looking liquid. Despite the appearance, it has had a most chequered career, being in and out of the good books of civilized company since day one.

Day one was probably one pleasant afternoon in the spring of 1612 or so, in Amsterdam. Doctor Sylvius — Sylvius was his professional name; his real one, Franciscus de la Boe, had less of a ring to it — was in his laboratory mixing and heating and cooling and bustling about. He was on the trail of a cure-all — something simple, cheap, pleasant, and universally effective against all ailments. He theorized on the diuretic value of the juniper berry, threw some grain alcohol into the retort, stirred (didn't shake) and when the smoke cleared, he had it.

"It" was called ginievre after the Dutch word for the juniper that imparted the taste, and that remains gin's principal flavoring agent today. Come Monday morning, Dr. Sylvius began dispensing it to all comers. Success was immediate. It cured people of things they hardly knew they had. Quite a pleasant cure it was, too, a bit of a buzz, a drowsy feeling, and then you got to lie down until dinnertime. Someone thought it would benefit the English soldiers fighting on the continental soil nearby. One way to fire up the men's morale was to dole out a few sips each day of Dr. Sylvius's finest. It gave a pleasant glow, a calm feeling, slurred speech, and a certain measure of courage.

Gin came to England to an eager welcome. William of Orange was busy becoming king in 1688, after James II fled across the Channel. Much of what England had been drinking had come from France, and William put a stop to that when France became the enemy. To offset the loss, he gave the English the right to manufacture their own spirits and passed along what he could recall of Dr. Sylvius's methods. An industry was born. Records indicate that gin consumption soared along a curve to gladden the heart of any corporate executive. Whereas 1690 saw half a million gallons sipped, in 1710 the total was 18 million gallons guzzled — three for every man, woman, and child in England. Queen Anne made a decisive move on gin tax that year. She lowered it. Even more people took to it, and public drunkenness became epidemic. In 1736 the Gin Act was passed, limiting production and imposing huge taxes. Needless to say, it didn't work. Gin was as easy to make as it was to drink. By 1742 it was truly a spirit of the people; moonshiners flourished, sales boomed, and hangovers (worse) multiplied. In frustration Parliament repealed the Gin Act, a retail licence dropped to one pound from the previous fifty quid, small charges were levied on manufacturers rather than on gin sellers, and everyone was happier.

Wretched most mornings, but happier the nights before.

Gin sold for next to nothing and was probably overpriced at that. In Gin Lane, it was a penny a glass. More, if you insisted the glass be rinsed. Gin was very much a drink for the common folk. Upper-class English disdained it, preferring to sip their hock or doctor their port and mull over what little claret they had left in the cellar, pining for about the good old days when they could get a decent little château for a shilling.

"This much reviled liquid is the most specially English of all spirits," the critic George Saintsbury said in its defence more than a century later, and gin came to take a turn towards respectability. In the ensuing years it proved itself an aid in the military once more, this time countering malaria. Granted, the quinine water really did the medical work, but the gin made the quinine taste better.

By 1920 gin was forbidden in America, but Prohibition found more of it being made than ever before. It required next to nothing to produce: some neutral grain spirits, a little flavoring, and an afternoon's effort. Inventory control was a joy — no sooner made than sold. In the thirteen years of Prohibition, millions of buckets, bottles, mason jars, and washtubs full were produced. When it was good, it was ghastly. When it was bad, it killed you. The line in "Button Up Your Overcoat" that went "Beware of bootleg hootch" wasn't just poetic licence. It was a health warning.

Prohibition too passed, like all bad dreams, and gin came back, stronger than ever. Only in the past few years has it showed signs of slipping from its perch atop the white spirits pyramid, losing some ground to a relative newcomer from Poland and Russia: vodka.

The most popular gin is dry gin, or London, English, or American gin. Dutch gin — Hollands, Genever, Schiedam — is another subject altogether. London dry gin begins as a mixture of roughly 75 percent corn, 15 percent barley malt, and 10 percent other grains. The mix is mashed, cooked, fermented, and distilled. The addition of distilled water reduces the high proof level, and then it's all distilled once again in a pot still, this time with the flavorings. These, called botanicals, are what give gin its delicate and distinctive taste. They vary from producer to producer, are kept strictly secret, and have one ingredient that's common to all: juniper berries. Otherwise, they consist of bark and peel and roots and berries: ginger and licorice, coriander, cassia, anise, caraway, lemon, orange peel, cacao nibs, and angelica root.

One of England's best-known gin producers, Tanqueray, still follows a centuries-old recipe unvaried since 1740, when Charles Tanqueray devised it. Today, insists his great-great-great-grandson, John Tanqueray, nothing is different, save the quality of the spirit alcohol, which is far better now, and the storing of the special ingredients in climate-controlled vaults. Tanqueray is understandably tight-lipped about those ingredients but allows that the company finds its coriander in Russia, juniper in Italy, and angelica root in Saxony. One of Tanqueray's secrets for gin's supreme dryness is maturation of the juniper berries. "They can make the gin oily and very perfumy," says J.T. "So we dry ours for two or three years before using them." Dryness is a holy quest for Tanqueray.

Age does nothing for gin. Today's hot-off-the-still gin is as good as the gin you've had in the cupboard since graduation. Theoretically, it will keep forever too. Once off the line, it is ready for drinking, making it one of the few alcoholic beverages of note in whose production man plays a more important role than nature.

The martini became gin's most famous byproduct. There are as many different martinis as there are martini drinkers. (A book called *268 Perfect Martinis* spends many pages on the subject; my recipe isn't among the 268.)

Beyond martinis, take some gin, add six drops of angostura bitters, and dilute to taste with fizzy mineral water and there's a pink gin. Take two parts grapefruit juice, one part gin, salt the rim of the glass, and sip a Salty Dog.

There are some truly wretched recipes about, and A Young Girl's Fancy leads the list. To serve six (young girls or other fanciful folk), you need two jiggers of gin, which you warm, adding a teaspoon of powdered sugar (your skin's starting to crawl already, right?), six peeled almonds, and a crushed peach kernel. (You can use, instead of the latter, a teaspoon of Crème de Noyaux, that somewhat vile sweet liqueur made from peach pits.) Cool the mixture, add a third of a jigger of kirsch, the same amount of peach brandy (stop that chattering of the teeth!), two jiggers dry vermouth, and four jiggers Sauternes or other sweet white wine (hell, you might as well go the bundle and use some muscatel!). Having managed to keep your head while mixing up all of this, you now shake it with ice and then strain.

Got to bed at once. Quite likely, without young girl!

Yet gin is best at its simplest. John Tanqueray taught me my favorite summertime drink: a goodly measure of Tanqueray, smoking on the rocks, with a sizable twist of orange. That's it — clean, delicious.

Gin remains with us, up and down in popularity and respectability, but always a favorite with someone. Good gin can be had in virtually every country. Only a few choose not to let it in for political or religious reasons.

And, for reasons no one is entirely sure of, you can't buy it in Mongolia. Inner or Outer. If you fancy a spot of mother's ruin as the sun makes its maddeningly slow transit off the yardarm, you may want to avoid the Ulan Bator Holiday Inn or the Sheraton in Iraq.

*M*artini Time

❦

─────────────────────────────────

*N*OW AND AGAIN, the question arises — often after a strenuous
wine tasting ("Adventures in Marinade": thirteen reds under six
bucks, and some of them worth half that, easily!) — something
like, "Where *did* the martini come from, anyway?" In the interest
of pure research, then, some answers while the tongue and
cheeks recover from the attack of megatannin.

The British say they did it first: the name, they claim, derives
from the Martini & Henry rifle and its accompanying kick. Not
convincing, but there are possibilities . . .

The Italians say no way. Martini & Rossi, the vermouth people, have to take credit for what was their idea all along: adding
vermouth to gin.

But only the California town of Martinez — sixty-four
kilometres across the bay from San Francisco — has an annual
festival, still going strong, that honors itself as the true birthplace
of The Martini. And if you think the last one a strange bartender
mixed for you wasn't dry enough, you should have tried the
original: gin mixed with Sauternes. After the initial spasms and
shuddering — voila! The Martinez Special, great-granddaddy of
the martini we know and love. And are loving more and more
these days; for a while there, wine had all but eclipsed mixed

drinks in popularity, and the aged-in-wood spirits weren't doing well.

But it all comes around again: vodka and gin were first, now malt whiskies are making a major comeback as well. One of the most entertaining of the new-bar-in-town phenomena is the page-after-page-of-martinis menu.

Back to California: same town, different scenario. Professor Jerry Thomas, one ace bartender in the 1880s, having already invented one cocktail that would assure him of immortality (naming it after himself, just to make sure: the Tom and Jerry), one sunny day faced a weary traveller, across his bar. The traveller needed a pick-me-up to keep on trucking — or the then-equivalent.

In 1882, Thomas went so far as to publish one of the early bartender's manuals, *The Bon Vivant's Companion*, in which pages he remembered the original recipe he whipped up that day:

1 dash bitters
2 dashes maraschino liqueur
1 wineglass vermouth
2-3 lumps of ice (the cubist period was still a way off)
1 pony of Old Tom gin (that's four-to-one, in favor of the vermouth by now!)
¼ lemon

Even with a *whole* lemon in there — and a couple of grape-fruit — it would still have been sweet as sin!

Martinis became the summer cocktail. For serious cocktail-hour observers, they're the *only* cocktail. And, after the white-wine-boom and the coolers scare, we're once again drinking cocktails at five o'clock.

For some members of the business community, martinis-for-lunch have never faded from fashion, but a whole new generation or three has just recently returned to the icy delights of the whiter-than-white mixed drink with, well, *something* afloat in it:

olives, lemon twist, orange peel, cocktail onions, even oysters or jalapeño peppers or cedar saplings.

More than any other mixed drink, it was the martini that made it all right to drink hard liquor in polite or mixed (or sometimes, although not necessarily, both) company. And gin was the catalyst, although that is changing, too, with vodka now another major contender.

For purists there's never been any question about the how and what: dry gin, a small amount of dry vermouth, an olive or a twist of lemon peel. *Nothing* else! In fact, gin, vermouth, and ice to chill it down while mixing are the three essentials. After that, it's all fancy-time.

You can't beat the old standards, the great classics: Caviar and champagne. Basic black and pearls. Blue blazer and grey flannels. Steak 'n' baked potato. Troilus and Cressida (who's ever heard of Troilus and Camry, I ask you?). And gin and vermouth. Always the same ingredients. Only the proportions and the flavoring/garnish change.

In the old regime, the regular Dry Martini went like this:

2 oz. dry gin
½ oz. dry vermouth
Green olive or a twist and that was immutable.

At least, till it got muted! These days, half an ounce of vermouth is practically drowning it, according to most. Some bartenders wield eyedroppers.

The Classic Martini stood unchallenged for years at:

2 parts dry gin
1 part vermouth
Dash of orange bitters

and should the proportions suddenly jump to seven-to-one and you've found an onion at the bottom, it just became a Gibson.

So who *did* invent the multiple-martini lunch? It probably invented itself, but it was JFK who first came up with the phrase, railing against business-dealings-at-the-expense-of-the-tax-payer. Remember?

George McGovern came up — short, as it turned out! — against the three-martini lunch; he downgraded his tirades to include two-martini lunches. Jimmy Carter did too. I don't recall Ronald Reagan's stand on the subject, and George Bush probably hasn't had time to take a position on it yet.

But other American presidents endorsed the martini. Roosevelt took two before dinner. Never three, never one. Two was the presidential number, and they each went like this:

4 parts gin
1 part vermouth

never more, never less.

Nixon once invited the Washington press corps upstairs (in the White House) and personally shook a few for the media to toast incoming 1971 when Watergate was still only an apartment building.

Me, I drink 'em just about any way they come. Now, with vodka on the rise as the main martini component, I even drink 'em that way. But it's nothing new. Back in *Casino Royale*, James Bond announced his procedure to a bartender:

Big champagne glass
3 parts Gordon's gin
1 part vodka
1 part Lillet (a French vermouth), shaken with ice until very cold
Large sliver of lemon peel

Whaddaya mean, stirred? Rent the video!
Why vodka? Sneaky reasons at first: simply to eliminate the

telltale odor of gin on the breath when people got back to the office. You could always tell multi-martini lunchers: they wobbled a little and had olive-breath!

Restaurants abound with specialty martini lists. But ask anyone in charge of a bar and you'll learn that vodka has taken the lead as the ingredient of choice.

My old friend John Tanqueray finds that troublesome. His T-martini remains my personal favorite:

> Smoky-cold ice cubes
> Zest of orange, squeezed over the ice
> Ice-cold gin to desired level
> Rumor of vermouth
> Stir fast, lose the ice, sip slowly

Tanqueray's own portable vermouth bottle has merely dropped a couple of millimetres in over thirty years of perfect-to-the-T making.

But if you can't beat 'em . . . Tanqueray vodka hit the shelves in Canada in 1990. It's probably just as well John T. has retired from his office on London's Goswell Road to his place in the country.

Smoked salmon? Jalapeño peppers? Scallops, caviar, loganberry liqueur, espresso, cranberry juice, star anise, cedar boughs? All that's the handiwork of one Adam Wensley, a whiz-about-booze who makes them up as he goes along as well as keeping track of all the old favorites. His domain is a Vancouver restaurant called The Raintree. It probably has the largest choice of offbeat martinis anywhere. If you sample a couple of standards and then go on to a third in the "weird" category, he'll call you adventuresome.

He'll also call you a cab, and that's the way it should be if you're going to enjoy the delights of the neo-martini!

*T*he World of Whiskies

———————— ❧ ————————

*T*AKE THE VERY WORD: whisky. It has become almost a generic term, denoting liquor — hard booze, drinking liquor. When we talk about whisky, generally we mean Scotland's greatest gift to the world: Scotch whisky. The Scots and the Irish have been kicking the concept around longer than anyone else. Today there is a big whisky business in Canada, the United States and Japan. It is also produced in Germany, Holland, Denmark, and Australia, and probably a lot of other places. One is Korea, home of the famous Korean Ginseng whisky.

Scotch leads the way in terms of popularity, sales, and diversity of styles. Basically, it is made from barley. Other whiskies are produced from corn, rye, wheat, oats, rice, millet, even Indian corn. The word *whisky* derives from the Gaelic *uisge beatha*, which the Scots and the Irish shortened to *usquebaugh*. Both mean water of life and there is to this day argument over who said it first. The English didn't feel like twisting their tongues around it so they came up with *whisky*.

An e or not an e? Canadian and Scotch whisky are customarily spelled the same way, without the e. The Irish keep it in their whiskey and the Americans used to. The BATF (Bureau of Alcohol, Tobacco and Firearms) leaves it out of its standards guides but does allow for it to be used if a distiller feels like it.

Every highland laird of any stature would have his own still, producing smoky, raunchy stuff for private consumption and colossal hangovers. The nice thing was the lack of taxation. In 1814 production of anything less than five hundred gallons per still was outlawed, which almost caused a revolution. The government managed to convince some of the less truculent highlanders to go into the whisky business and produce it under supervision, selling it legally. The whisky industry was born, and the world's a better place for all that.

There are two basic types of whisky (three, if you count grain whisky) — malts and blends. The principal areas of production are the Scottish highlands, the lowlands, Islay, and Campbeltown; each is known for a whisky that's individual in taste and style, production methods and techniques.

The five production stages common to all whisky are malting, mashing, fermenting, distilling, and maturing — and blending if, and as, required. The process is simple and natural enough: grain is spread on the floor of the malt house, sprinkled with warm water, and after a couple of weeks the seeds germinate and sprout. It is now known as malt. The malt is moved onto a screen above a peat fire, whose smoke gives the grain its characteristic flavor. (Lowlands have less smokiness than highlands; Campbeltown and Islay tend to roast theirs a great deal more.) The dried grain is ground to grist in the mill room and then mixed with warm water in a mash tun. Sugar is produced from the starches, and the water is drawn off. The mixture is now known as wort. Into the fermenting vats it goes next, and cultivated yeast is added to produce alcohol and carbon dioxide. This process done, the substance is called wash or beer. Pot stills produce a low-alcohol distillate known as low wines, the first and last parts of which — head and tails — are known as feints and are separate from the stuff in the middle, the useful spirit that is now whisky. Off into casks, which can hold anywhere from 35 to 130 gallons. The size of the cask is determined solely by convenience. That's one of the few things about whisky production not nailed down as law.

Water is added to bring the proof level down, and one Dr. Schidroweitz once stated that the best water is that which "has its origin as a spring served with water which has passed through a red granite formation and which, after rising from its source, passes through peaty country."

On to the business of malts and blends. Before 1853 all Scotch was single malt whisky, meaning unblended spirit. The firm of Andrew Usher was the first to begin blending malt with grain whisky (made mostly from corn and a small amount of sometimes unmalted barley, produced in the patent or continuous still by distillers in lower Scotland). Initially there was a very practical reason: reduction of production costs and creation of a lighter, sipping spirit.

Today, the vast majority of whisky sold in North America is blended. The difference is often in the proportion of the four types of malt. Highlands is considered the finest (and costliest), possessing only a little smoke. Banffshire, Glenlivet, and Spey-side regions produce the acknowledged best. Lowlands malt is also quite light and maybe even less smoky; Campbeltown is very full and heavy with smoke, and Islay is pungent and extremely smoky.

Highland and lowland whiskies are ready in six to eight years as a rule; others benefit from more ageing, and a dozen years seems the right time. Many whiskies are aged far longer. In the past few months, I sampled varieties of Glen Grant eight, twelve, twenty-one, even forty-one years old. The twelve-year-old pleased my nose and palate most; by the time I arrived at forty-one, the whisky had come around to being very woody and surprisingly harsh.

In Scotland today there are 130 distillers: 95 highland, 11 lowland, 8 Islay, and 2 Campbeltown; 14 others produce grain whisky. From this 130 come more than four thousand different brands and blends.

Talisker is a sumptuous malt from the town of Carbost on the Isle of Skye. From its picturesque distillery on the shores of Loch

Harpot, Talisker makes its way, in small amounts, around the world. The distillery was founded in 1830 by Hugh and Kenneth Macaskill. A parish minister, the Reverend Roderick MacLeod, was hardly happy about it. He decried its establishment as being "one of the greatest curses that, in the ordinary course of Providence, could befall this or any other place," according to the *New Statistical Account of Scotland*, 1843. Despite some setbacks, the whisky from Talisker acquired a resounding reputation, to the point where Robert Louis Stevenson felt compelled to mention it in a poem: "The king o'drinks, as I conceive it, Talisker, Isla or Glenlivet."

Today most Talisker whisky goes into blending, but a proportion of the make is bottled as a single malt, proudly given the Talisker name and marketed by the Distillers Agency Ltd. of Edinburgh. "The golden spirit of the Isle of Skye" lives on to the delight of those who have access to it.

One spring, Richard Greenbank of the James Buchanan Company guided me through a distillery in the castle town of Linlithgow, a pleasant drive out of Edinburgh, to visit with distillery manager Ian Garden and learn about the whisky business firsthand. Garden's knowledge was matched only by Greenbank's enthusiasm.

After learning about whisky, and sharing a dram to acknowledge the passing of the morning, on to lunch at the famous Champany Restaurant. It is a place I can recommend highly; lunch was roast guinea fowl, prawn-and-mussel salad, veal with nutmeg and orange and a tomato purée sauce, and a fair bit of Black and White. Make a note of it if you're travelling to Edinburgh. This charming establishment specializes in game according to season. Phone Philipstown 532.

Let's look at Irish whiskey. The principal popular misconception about it, cobwebby by now, is that Irish whiskey is made from potatoes. Not so. The Irish haven't produced whiskey from potatoes for years and years — if, indeed, they ever did. As elsewhere in the whiskey-making world, it is produced from grain. Perhaps the myth began because distilled whiskey is often called poteen, the name deriving from the pot still. You can buy poteen for home consumption if you're Irish or brave, and ideally both. It's clear, as flavorless as it is colorless, a lot like vodka, and it does tend to wallop the unwary drinker. It can be had in Chicago, New York, and San Francisco.

Irish whiskey is the fermented mash of malted barley and unmalted corn, rye, wheat and oats. Although it is "smoked" like many other whiskies, no smoke actually comes into contact with the whiskey; smokeless anthracite is now frequently used for the process instead of peat. Pot stills produce the main quantity of the spirit; a few column stills yield a lighter style.

The other great whiskey of the world is American whiskey, better known as bourbon. Farmers of Scottish, Irish, and Dutch origin were the originators of this particular substance. Successful distilling, as usual, was merely a matter of moving out of the reach of the tax man. George Washington wasn't only the father of his country; he was also the originator of the whiskey excise tax in 1791. So, off went the disgruntled whiskey makers into Indian territory where few folk would follow and where there was good water (lots of limestone formations) and access to grain. Stills sprang up in Indiana and Kentucky. The first to get a viable cottage industry going was a man of the cloth, the good Rev. Elijah Craig, who operated in Georgetown, Bourbon County. Hence the name bourbon whiskey; it could just as easily have come down to us georgetown or even craig whiskey.

Here, corn was much more plentiful than rye, so corn mash was the principal ingredient. People were, I presume, not so much concerned with the taste as with — like Dr. Johnson and his port — the effect.

To make bourbon, corn is ground and cooked, then malt and yeast are added and off it all goes into a double-column or patent still. Nowadays, deionized water is added to reduce proof without adding undesired minerals to the spirit. Maturation takes place in new charred white oak barrels. No one is sure why charred oak is preferable, but there's conjecture that an accidental fire along the way made a whiskey taste especially good. The two production styles are sweet and sour-mash. In the first, cultivated or fresh yeast is used. Sour-mash depends on the yeast-back process, working from previous fermentations in much the same way as sourdough bread is made. The three basic bourbon types are straight, blended, and light.

Japanese whiskey is an interesting product: fairly sweet, medium weight. Many who taste it blind consider it both agreeable and distinctive. Suntory is a blend, made from both pot-still and continuous-still production, using malted barley, millet, corn, rice, and even Indian corn.

Welsh whiskey comes in stone crocks like the old ginger beer bottles, and it's surprisingly light to my palate. It strikes me as a novelty whiskey, not terribly interesting. But Manx whiskey is something else again. I loved it so much after finding it in England not long ago that I carted some home and rationed it carefully. Glen Kella is the name of the whiskey, and it comes in a square-shouldered bottle very much like Bushmill's. It is slightly sweet, mellow, full and delicate, rolling around the tongue for a long time; it has become one of my favorite sipping whiskies. Since none was available in Canada, I sent off a special order. My cautious order for two cases of Glen Kella came back annotated to the effect that the distiller wouldn't ship quantities of less than a hundred cases. (I wouldn't have thought they'd produce much more than that, but there you are. Maybe the citizens of Man are great domestic whisky-fanciers.)

Glen Kella can be had by the glass at Jake O'Shaughnessy's in Seattle, which enjoyable restaurant and bar claims to possess the world's largest selection of liquors. Having myself counted forty-seven malt whiskies at the bar, they can have that claim by me!

Scotland produces a number of specialty whiskies. James Buchanan makes Royal Household for the royal family, although I have seen some for sale on occasion. There are anniversary and commemorative bottlings and vattings, plus all those odd-shaped bottles and decanters: curling rocks and stags, sculptures and ceramic jugs, minis and maxis. I have in my cabinet two bottles of Glen Grant's Royal Wedding Whisky, a somewhat costly novelty that was briefly available in Britain in very limited supplies. This was a special vatting for the marriage of Prince Charles and Lady Diana. No, their picture isn't on the label (that alone may make it unique, the only British product during the wedding that didn't carry the photo). It's "a whisky specially blended from two vattings of Glen Grant, 1948 and 1961." It's quite lovely stuff. No Royal Baby Whisky to date.

A general word on ageing: Whisky's age is of interest, of course; the label tells how long the product has been in wood. But whisky ages only in the barrel and not in the bottle; there's no point in keeping any lying about the place. Well, perhaps as an inflation-hedge . . .

If you arrange a comparative tasting of Scotch, keep in mind you don't sip it. Rather "nose" it for the bouquet, the aroma, the smokiness, the total effect. That frustrating experience is best dispensed with quickly; then you get on with sipping the one you liked best.

All this fancy about clear spirits and white wines and light-is-right has cut into the demand. But the enterprising Scots have been about this business a good long time, and I'm sure they'll turn that trend around too. Even if the world should give up on Scotch entirely, there is still Mrs. Fraser, who may be counted on to come to the rescue of the economy even after North Sea oil gives out. Mrs. Fraser owns Moniack Castle in northern Scotland, and she and her family produce red, white, and rosé wines. Emboldened by the success of a family hobby, Mrs. Fraser has decided to give the drinking world another original gift — she has recently announced the imminent production of a birch-flavored wine made according to a Scottish recipe her family has been jealously guarding for centuries.

It may not prove to have much bouquet, but there's bound to be a hell of a bark to it!

Our own Canadian rye is always blended, and cereal grains only are used. None of ours reaches consumers in less than three years, and export rye is always six years old or more, with the States being the prime buyer. Because it's called rye, many people think only rye is used, but corn wheat and barley malt can also be ingredients, with specific proportions being the trade secret of each distiller. If you like CC better than VO, that's your palate responding to some of those proportions and subtleties. Any loss of rye whisky due to evaporation — what the cognac producers call the angel's share — must be made up by adding new whisky. That rule is specific to Canadian whisky production, and it's an expensive one, of course (others often add water).

Canadian whisky is virtually our national drink — Bob and Doug MacKenzie notwithstanding — rye and water, rye and ginger, and (shudder) rye and Coke. Although we consider ourselves real rye drinkers, especially in middle Canada, we're really real Canadian-whisky drinkers. After all, CC and VO and Wiser's and OFC you know by name, but when's the last time you drank some Quaker or Rittenhouse, or made a Manhattan with Meadowbrook or Old Overholt? Those are rye whiskies — *real* ryes, deep and tasty, a little heavy, American-made, same proof level as bourbon, minimum of two years in charred oak and a minimum of 51 percent rye instead of corn. Real rye drinkers claim that's the only way to make a Manhattan — never mind your lighter, smoother Canadian whisky. There are few real rye drinkers around our parts, and few real ryes available in Canada.

The principal characteristics of Canadian whisky are lightness and a delicacy of flavor and body. "If you aren't exactly wild about the taste of whisky," states one of my reference volumes, "Canadian whisky may be your spirit — it's the lightest-bodied, mellowest of them all." There's that word *light*, which crops up all over with reference to the world's wines and spirits these days. It's important to remember that Canadian is 100 percent grain whisky, which differentiates it from so-called light whiskies made in America. Those are produced by adding neutral, flavorless grain spirits to the blend to achieve the desired level of lightness. Another book describes Canadian as "distinctive and decorous," the latter hardly a word I've ever thought of in the bars and lounges of the prairies! "There is no great difference in Canadian whiskies [of the same proof]," the same book continues somewhat offhandedly. "They are virtually indistinguishable from one another — therefore, buy the most economical." Obviously not the words of a loyal Canadian whisky drinker.

Brand loyalty is a big thing in Canadian whisky; people insist on their CC and soda no matter where they go. Unfortunately for the industry, light spirits and wine have made dramatic raids on the total consumption, especially in terms of premium-priced products, and a good number of people have been switching to a lower category. It may all point to a potential problem: an inventory of very old, very fine Canadian whiskies building up in Ontario.

More than fifty Canadian whiskies are produced in Ontario alone, by more than two dozen distillers. A close examination, though, reveals a network of subsidiaries and a short list of major players in the business, including Hiram Walker and Seagram's, Schenley's and Standard Brands, Gilbey's and National Distillers, Brown-Foreman (who export, in bulk, all that Canadian Mist), and a handful of independents, among them Potter's and Otto Rieder's Grimsby-based Rieder distilleries, which also makes all of those fine eaux-de-vie.

The costliest Canadians are Crown Royal, Schenley's Order of Merit, and Wiser's Oldest — eighteen years old, and for my palate the nicest Canadian whisky, with Alberta Springs Sipping Whisky another favorite. Next in price, the popular premiums: CC, VO, OFC, Wiser's Deluxe, and more.

J.P. Wiser's oft-repeated adage was that "horses should hurry but whisky should take its time." Wiser was a Pennsylvania Dutch descendant who settled in Ontario in the middle of the past century. Here there was no civil war, nor (as yet) any thought of prohibition. Like other major names in the budding whisky business — Henry Corby, Joseph Seagram, Hiram Walker, James Worts, and William Gooderham — Wiser found his way into the business of distilling as a logical progression from the business of grain handling and milling, or cattle raising.

Gooderham and Worts established the first Canadian distillery of significance, on the Toronto waterfront. Corby created Corbyville on the Moira River, about eight kilometres from Belleville, Ontario, in 1859. Then as now, his company provided transportation to and from the distillery for its workers, tea and milk for their refreshment, and even some company housing. Shortly after the First World War, Corby's and Wiser's joined forces in Corbyville, where the good water was. Wiser's Deluxe and Wiser's Oldest are still produced there.

So much Canadian whisky is exported south of the border — in bulk as well as bottle — that there are numerous brands whose names we neither recognize nor ever see on our own shelves. CC and VO and Wiser's are the big international names, and so is Windsor Canadian. Other big sellers across the border have such names as King's Crest and Old Mr. Boston, Canadian River, Laird's Premium and Canadian Breeze, MacNaughton and the huge-selling Canadian Mist. There are James Foxe and Grande Canadian (take that, Bill 101). There's even Paddington of Canada.

Officially, our leading customer says that "Canadian whisky is a distinctive product of Canada, manufactured in compliance with the laws of the Dominion of Canada and . . . containing no distilled spirits less than three years old. Canadian whisky is blended whisky and shall not be designated as straight." That's from U.S. federal regulations. Canadian law states that it is to be produced from cereal grains only and that the youngest whisky in the blend can not be younger than whatever age is stated on the label. It has to have a minimum of three years in forty-gallon oak barrels, and then it can go into the world, but if it's less than four years old when sold it has to say so on the label. Virtually all Canadian whisky is six years old or more when marketed. Canadian Club is a six-year-old, VO and OFC are eight, Crown Royal and Wiser's are ten.

Although the excise people look after the customary collection of taxes, the government, surprisingly, has never set many other limitations on Canadian whisky production: grain formulas, distilling proof, special ageing, cooperage — all that is more or less left up to the distiller. The government seems to believe, even more surprisingly, that the distillers are better judges of what the public, both at home and abroad, wants in a whisky. It's a type of government thinking that seems to have escaped virtually any other application. But then, most of the major names in Canadian whisky have been around longer than the Canadian government. Any Canadian government.

*D*on't Waste the Champagne!

———❦———

WAS THERE EVER an occasion, however glorious, however mundane, that wasn't accented, augmented, and just generally raised heavenward on those upwardly mobile, happy little bubbles of the sublime Champagne?

Pour me that other glass and I can sit here and write stuff like that all afternoon. Champagne is the wine of legend and celebration of lovers — or at least very good friends; of all-round, pure (if sometimes heavily-mortgaged) pleasure.

What a waste it has been, all those bottles of good bubbly spilling down the fronts of ships. Good thing the christening trend hasn't carried over to all the other things being proudly built today; we would find people hurling magnums of Nova Scotia champagne at every condo-convert opening in the neighborhood. Actually, I don't really have a quarrel with the practice of having Champagne on hand for occasions that can even remotely be construed as special. But let's save some of the stuff for sipping. What's wrong with smashing a bottle of rye over the bow of the MV Marginal Belle?

We were sitting around in front of the season's first fire the other night, just me and the cats, trying to get up an excuse to open the last bottle of Champagne in the house. (The Champagne-man drops off four quarts every Tuesday and Thursday and this was a Wednesday, you understand!) The topic of conversation turned to all those funny names people have given to Champagne bottles over the years: splits and Rehoboams, tappit-hens and Salmanazars. Why, we wondered, was it that all the odd-sized bottles were named after old Babylonians? What would happen if our domestic producers, with the almost certain approval of Mel Hurtig, adopted a uniquely Canadian version of that policy?

"I'll have a Trudeau of Baby Duck," people would say. "So long as you're up, get me one of them Clarks of Chateau Nougat Sparkling Broccoli. Have one yourself, too."

"At Blanche's wedding, they served seven Mulroneys of Old Niagara Revisionist. We haven't seen the groom since."

The one that has a real ring of authority to it would have to be the Diefenbaker. "We've got six Diefenbakers of Osoyoos Brut in the cellar. We're waiting for it to become stable."

Have you every wondered what each of those champagne bottle terms means, in reference to size and serving? Here's a list. Since most people still think in terms of the old English measures with regard to wines and spirits, we've decided, just this once, to recall days gone by.

Name	Size	Oz.	Glasses
Split	1/2 pint	6-1/2	2
Half bottle	4/5 pint	13	3-1/2
Full bottle	4/5 quart	26	5
Magnum	2 btls.	52	10
Jeroboam	4 btls.	104	21
Tappit-hen	5 btls.	128	26
Rehoboam	6 btls.	156	31
Methuselah	8 btls.	208	41
Salmanazar	12 btls.	312	62
Balthazar	16 btls.	416	83
Nebuchadnezzar	20 btls.	520	104

These extra-size bottles are handfilled very carefully and want to be opened the same way. Oh yes, there was an even bigger bottle than the Nebuchadnezzar: a one-of-a-kind, five-foot-tall model that was flown from France for the 1976 opening bash at the Tavern-on-the-Green in New York.

I haven't the faintest idea who poured. Arnold Schwarzenegger, maybe?

PART TWO

Life with the Cats

Observations from Floor-Level: Kitty Get Down

———————————🍒———————————

*T*HERE WEREN'T always The Cats.

Nor were they capitalized, at first. As they do to most of us, the cats came in the night: first, as kittens carried home in a box from the house of friends who were filled with glee and rid of guilt. "It's so nice they found a good home" actually means "We're so glad we got rid of them without denting our conscience."

And so they came in a box marked Washington Apples; two of them, orange and white and taking over from the very beginning. Big Time Fred and Bradley (named after Barbara Stanwyck).

Taking Over is high among the things The Cats do best; along with intense sleeping and bobbing for gerbils at Hallowe'en, which we no longer let them do; you've got to draw a line somewhere. Anytime you need anything taken over, call a cat. Had Campeau had a cat to consult, things might have been different. I have read nothing to the effect, but I suspect Conrad Black has a cat on his payroll. Want to learn how to do an effective takeover, so the take-ees don't know what's hitting them? Consider the ways of the cat, my MBA, and be wise — he toils not, neither does he spin; just blinks a little and purrs his way right into your will.

Shortly after the initial takeover came the first of the mergers. From out of October's misty dark, crossing the sisal welcome mat on the front porch with a lazy stretch, came the famous Quincy — named after Anthony Quinn — who stayed for a total of twenty-three years, which is a longer time than I have yet spent with any other sentient being. Then Smallcreep and Freezegreen and Fat Margaret and MacDuff; Max the Manx — shortest term of them all — and Minnie and Muscat and Sandor and Clint and Thurston and all the rest. Finally, Herbie the Screamer and the keepers thereof. Along with the Willis Point Fire Department, he gets a Friday night sign-off credit on DiscDrive. And why not? Poor fat furbucket doesn't get much else: Melitta scoop of scientifically formulated cat-crunch in response to his screamage, couple of times a day. What kind of life is that?

I guess there always *have* been The Cats.

But they're like, I dunno, your *kids* or something, people mutter in high miffage. Not mine, they're not. I can't abide people who anthropomorphicate their cats and do all that cute bit. Kittens are cute. For about a week — until they shred your first silk tie. Cats are not cute. Cats are a lot of things, but surprisingly short on cute. Cute are people who make them pop out of adorable little books by British publishers or photograph them hanging from clotheslines draped in spaghetti.

Not mine, you don't. The little dears will shred your forearm first as would be only fitting.

What The Cats mostly are is company. They have their moments and they don't so much interact with you and your life, they tesseract it. What other creatures can you think of that take dental flossing to a level of high art, perched there, on the bathroom sink, trying to stimulate their little gums? You ever see a budgie floss? Will you ever forget that moment of time-stopped-in-the-middle-of-its-otherwise-inexorable-Wellsian-passing when the cat-she's-still-a-kitten-to-me comes home one night from heaven knows what down at the school gym and asks if you think it's time she started shaving her legs?

Food plays a prominent part in their lives, as it does in yours and mine. "Oh no! The cats are cooking dinner tonight " is an observation of mixed apprehension and incredulity which I share many an evening with half a million of you who happen to have your radios tuned to DiscDrive. But the Almond Roca omelettes are starting to lose their appeal; after the first thirty or forty I just knew they would. Fondues are worse, and don't they love them. The hot oil spatters their fur and leaves little holes so they look like a second-hand football coat for one of those garden gnomes; there's an oil slick over the Axminster before the night is out. It isn't that the sloppiness of little paws clamoring for fondue morsels is innately troublesome. It's just that some of the entomological specimens they like to spear cause the other guests anxiety.

There are small moments when you feel very close to them and they don't even know it. Neither do you. Repainting their room while they're off at Siamese immersion camp for the summer. Taking the training wheels off the bicycle. Tying two skateboards together to accommodate all four limbs. Defrosting the fridge and finding those gerbils . . .

They watch too much TV, of course, who doesn't? I try to limit it and I'm concerned about the violence, too. Then they borrow the car and comes the first time being busted for a little indiscretion with a half gram of catnip in the backseat.

Oh yes, they are a major part of my life and, no, they're nothing at all like children. I wouldn't trade those moments for the world: the grad photos, the yearbook, the Kiwanis music festival semifinals. The mumps. Ever see a cat with mumps? It's like Dizzy Gillespie with fur on!

And still people say: but what do they do for you? It's got nothing to do with doing. They just are. Everybody else *does*. The government, the bus driver, the postie, the department store clerks, the checkouts at the supermarket, the veterinarian, the fitness instructor, the whole lot — they're the doers. The Cats are simply the be-ers. I don't need them to do anything for me at all; I have somebody who comes in four, five times in my life, does that for me.

I just like being with Them. They are better at it — being The Cats — than most of us are at being whatever it is we are. That may not be quite strong enough to call a philosophy, but religions have been founded on scantier premises. They weren't always The Cats, no. Before that there were some primordial hydrogen atoms . . .

Metamorphosis on a Theme of Tuna

———————❦———————

*T*HE DOMESTIC CAT'S ROLE in the development of music has generally been overlooked by musicologists. Tending to dismiss such compositions as "The Cat's Fugue" as indulgent curiosities has done little to secure for these talented furry creatures a permanent position in *Grove's*.

How many people, for instance, know about the all-cat orchestra of Mannheim? At the beginning of the seventeenth century, when the musical expression of the day was filled with flourish and embellishment, several cats took it upon themselves to counter these excesses with a return to simple, direct melodic development. The all-cat orchestra was formed in Mannheim as a result and received an annual stipend from both German and Austrian royalty, who were vying with one another for the favors of the ensemble. The segregationist policies of the group did give rise to controversy, and shortly thereafter a splinter group was born, augmenting the ranks of the felines with roosters, dogs, and the like. Since there was little demand for the aberrant group in Mannheim, they relocated in Bremen, where they enjoyed considerable public acclaim and got a recording contract.

According to Slonimsky, many famous composers have been accused of making cat sounds in their music. Bizet and Liszt, Chopin and Strauss, and of course Wagner, Varèse, and Schoenberg — all came under attack. However, in their own music, on which precious little scholarly comment exists, the cats have retaliated by utilizing composers' names in their own particular form of invective.

Orange Julius, one of the leading writers of the time, claimed that a performance of the "Symphonic Metamorphosis on a Theme of Tuna" had all the elegance of "Liszt in heat," apparently a frequent occurrence for that particular composer. Later, "Kitten on the Keys" was dismissed as being the "product of an immature mind, not unlike Beethoven with a headache chasing field mice."

History is generally silent on the subject of Bach's cat. Not only did the great composer father an inordinate number of children; he also carried a large tabby around with him in a bread basket, all through Leipzig. (In all fairness it should be pointed out that while Bach had a cat, he also had a duck and a six-pack of gerbils.)

There is no doubt that Bach was one of the greatest of all composers, but it is also worth noting that he was an extraordinarily talented cat trainer. Each morning he would give the cat a few guilders or gold crowns and send him off to the corner to buy a paper. The cat sometimes squandered the money on jujubes and didn't return until spring. But most of the time by noon or one o'clock, Bach could be observed sitting on the porch with a *Cuba Libre*, reading through the Hapsburg's gossip column and trying to make sense out of the by-now tattered stockmarket quotations.

Bach's cat also played excellent canasta, learned to serve champagne in a restaurant, and, later in life, dabbled in neurosurgery. But perhaps the most amazing achievement of this animal was that Bach had taught him to make spaetzle. So, on a Friday night, after a hard day of writing fugues, Bach would call over a couple of friends to while away the evening. I remember dropping in one night. I'd sold him a used clavichord that summer, and we had become friends.

I walked in the kitchen and there, to my surprise, was Bach's cat, his arms covered in flour, rolling spaetzle on a wooden board. The cat took my coat and wig, got me comfortable in the den, poured me a hefty daiquiri, and said that Bach would be down shortly. I could hear the master upstairs, finishing off BWV 656. Anna Magdalena was quilting a large tea cosy by the fire, and a couple of the boys were playing on the floor. Carl Philipp Emanuel wanted to borrow the virginal for a date, and Anna Magdalena gave him the keys and told him to have it home by ten.

I lit a cigar. The cat came in from the kitchen, stoked the fire, and offered a tray of shortbread. The spaetzle, he said, would be ready in about an hour.

Bach came down the stairs all hearty and full of good humor because he'd cleared Sunday's cantata out of the way. We discussed politics and Rhine vintages and got pretty jolly over a bottle of Siebenzwergenthaler Spätlese.

Around eight-thirty the cat announced dinner, and we sat down to spaetzle, wild mushrooms, venison, and a terrific dessert, the recipe of which I forgot to ask for. I left around midnight; the stars were out and the night was warm, so I walked home.

I'll never forget turning to wave. There in the doorway stood the greatest composer of all time, his family, and a cat that could make spaetzle, waving back.

*D*ie Fledermaus und MacPherson

———————————❦———————————

I HAVE BEEN TALKING to a prominent manufacturer of cat food to see if the company will put up some money to stage my opera, in which a cat takes a lead role. The company showed some initial scepticism, opining that there was little demand for a feline opera. Still, after showing them some notes and singing them a few bars from the opening aria, they seemed to show a glimmer of interest at least.

The libretto is based on original material from the Sidney and Eastern Railroad timetable, rewritten by me to the point of unrecognizability and to avoid paying royalties. The music is drawn at random from a variety of sources, including some I Ching computations. (Aha, you say, he owes a debt to John Cage. Well, maybe I do, but it's only about six bucks and besides, it was his turn to buy lunch anyway.)

Hebridean folk chants, bootleg Johnny Mathis albums, and works of such lesser-known classical composers as Pixie Ilyich Handbite and Andromeda Meerschaum make up the material. (Meerschaum, by the way, was the first Italian female composer to gain international recognition. It was for sheet-metal sculpture, but it's a start, isn't it?)

I digress.

In fact, that's the opening aria, sung by MacPherson, a young

Scots cat with a degree in oceanography as he bounds through the heather on a stultifyingly misty morning, keeping a keen ear out for the skirl of the pipes and a broken-down distillery left to him by his uncle Natchez.

As MacPherson approaches the legendary Loch Ness, he sees something. A couple of kilometres down the road he sees something else. Is there no stopping this cat's amazing powers of observation? The answer is no.

Late that night, stopping at the Blood Pudding Inn, the cat falls in love with a charming barmaid who doesn't have a name, but he doesn't hurt himself.

During the night, a giant bat (German: *grosse Batte*) appears to the cat in a dream, and the lovely duet "What's going on here?" is heard. Shortly thereafter, the curtain falls, and repeated efforts fail to revive it. During the ensuing intermission, patrons are forcibly restrained from leaving the concert hall.

The orchestra takes this opportunity to slip into something more comfortable, and Act 2 finds the locale has shifted. It is now over in the corner by those large ominous black speakers. A dog dances the charming entr'acte "I shouldn't be here, but it's a living," during which MacPherson is held down by two nuns to avoid an ugly scene in front of the curtain.

As the curtain opens again, we see that MacPherson has used up all of his lives and died mysteriously. He is in heaven and finds himself lounging on a chesterfield stuffed with catnip, and some pretty embarrassing stuff goes on while the cat makes a fool of himself to an instrumental interlude by the woodwinds. MacPherson is surrounded by the four angels of the apocalypse, Nina, Pinta, Santa Maria, and Morris, who entreat him to join them in a little six-pack bezique.

MacPherson doesn't reply, with the stirring aria "Take a card, any card." The recitative "Public Ordinance No. 4599 forbids gambling on any government-licensed carrier" rouses the orchestra out of its lethargy, and there is some pretty fast fiddling from the second violins as they try to catch up.

With everybody trading fours at the end, MacPherson having treed the dog in the foyer and the four angels trying to get off on the catnip, the police are called in.

When dawn finally comes, about an hour late, several Rhine maidens can be seen swimming in the distance and popping a lot of Henkell Trocken corks against the proscenium. The curtain falls to thunderous applause and there is nothingness.

I don't know, it's really more of a masque, I guess. Maybe Richard Bonynge can do something with it. Except he refuses to return my calls.

A elurobilia for the Family

———————— ❦ ————————

*D*ESPITE HOW WE ALL FELT last January when the oil truck couldn't get up the lane and the alder cache had all but run out, spring would seem to be at least approaching that corner, preparatory to being just around it. (No, it doesn't scan that well, but I'm sure Lorenz and Hart could have made it work.)

Besides crocuses and little buds on the tree you almost cut down because your cousin Deanna said it was dead and she's the one with the green thumb in the family, there's another sure-fire telltale sign. The cats get twitchy.

Instead of seeking out your dark brown cashmere sweater and claiming it for sleeping purposes, they look out the window, eyeing the new crop of robins much as a training-camp sergeant surveys the raw recruits. Rather than clawing their way up and down your tuxedo in the good-clothes closet (funny, it never used to be grey before, and now it looks perforated, like a Tetley teabag!), they wear the newel-post on the hall staircase into a rapier-thin toothpick-like affair.

They take to sitting on the back porch at inconvenient hours, tuning their banjos, declaiming the particular feline blues they so deeply feel, and staging nightly raids on the lair of the next-door Siamese, accompanied by a great deal of alarum and not nearly enough exeunting.

This past spring, Fat Margaret managed to knock a twenty-kilo television set onto the floor in a frenzy to approach Morris, who was starring in one of his triumphs on Channel 4: Tuna-with-Egg Commercial, The Sequel.

Margaret confided to me, as I swept the pieces out the door, she cowering under the chesterfield that has even more weight than she possesses after all, that although he's a dream she is sure his voice is dubbed — probably by Marni Nixon, the tape slowed down a little. Even Fellini does that, she told me thoughtfully, between bites at the carpet.

The cats are essentially quiet, save for the odd little war in the roses being fought just under the bedroom window. The neighborhood dogs, on the other hand, come spring, commence their alpine echo call-and-response number for another season.

You know how that goes: one self-appointed canine twit-muezzin (I'm sort of hoping to get the Ayatollah — any Ayatollah — to condemn this book and put a contract out on me so we can get some good press on it) starts the cry about four-thirty in the morning, and by five the whole street's up, all calling incomprehensible things to one another. I'll be glad when they get the prices of portable phones down to a level where the dogs can start to afford them.

To counter this still-noisy practice, I have dug out a recording of the Somerset and Dorset Railway — one of those old age of steam LPs that have become available in terrifying CD digital sound. I found some outdoor speakers too, the kind that Hammacher Schlemmer sells that will stun piranhas under water and never need servicing except for a little ScotchGuard and Lemon Pledge now and again.

Now, when the doggies get at it, I flick a switch in my sleep and a freight thunders up the street, through the garden, across the Bronsons' lawn, over the hedge, and into the Filipones' yard. The doggies shut up.

The neighbors are sure they have a case of the world's first steam-driven ghost, and the phenomenon is being investigated jointly by Hans Holzer and the International Brotherhood of Railway Engineers.

At any rate, apart from the occasional summit meeting under the windowbox around midnight, the furries that run around your house, or the ones running around mine, anyway, tend to keep more or less mum. They don't bark at the mailman. They don't roam the streets in packs looking for a fight outside the pool hall. They don't even play pool. And they almost never play their stereos loud after eleven.

What few overnight visitors they entertain tend to be models of discretion, tiptoeing in and out on little fog feet, checking out the left-over surprise du chef or whatever was in the bowl last night, and then settling down to a ritual bath on top of the black slacks that just came back from the cleaners. That sort of thing.

If you are a confirmed aelurophile, the sound of your neighbor's neurotic poodle in full Bidu Sayo imitation just after you've said goodnight to Johnny or David can be unsettling.

According to my lawyer, a felinist herself, there is a law that forbids a dog to bark a lot. Does it have teeth? The dog does — this we know from that night you stumbled across the neighbor's latter-day Victory Garden (there's a victory somewhere in the world every eleven seconds) in your stocking feet (you were trying to be very quiet on the flagstones after that muscatel tasting, remember?) — but the law is something else. It might get a little messy, what with having to find a couple of strong-minded complainers willing to risk the unending ire of both poodle and poodlette.

If your cat should ever get into a shouting match with that horrible Siamese from across the way, there could be countersuits. Go ahead, countersue, make my day, you say, because there's not a thing anybody can do about cat noise. Who says? Well, only King Henry V, is all. Cats can be noisy, cats don't need a licence, and there's the full clout of Hank the Five behind it.

With that sort of power you could probably organize a shape-note singing festival for the cats if you wanted to. Ah, sweet impunity, thy name is felis.

Apparently, we are all but powerless to license cats because of a decree handed down by Henry V, who reigned from 1413 to 1422. Now that may have been only nine years but cats all over the world, and ever since, refer to it as the Nine Golden Goodies. Some think that it may well be where and when this whole nine lives business originated.

When British granaries were being threatened by rats and mice wise old Henry ruled that "cats can roam free in Britain through all perpetuity." And apparently, singing, shouting, dancing, brawling in pubs, and driving straight-piped Camaros are included in that, if you're a cat.

They don't write laws like that anymore. Because Canada still follows British common law — much of Canada, much of it common — we are still abiding by what the Americans fought like all get-out to get away from. You might point that out to your good-for-nothing cat, the one who likes to go to Windsor and Buffalo and Blaine, just for personal safety's sake.

Here, the federal government can control cats and only on such lands as army camps and the like. It's just as well. After the GST furore, they don't need anything really serious like this to get involved with.

I have been asked by Fat Margaret and her circle of felinists to see if I can swing some weight about getting a good monthly cat glossy going, featuring foldouts of fish in the centre. (Well, first of all I have been asked to stop calling her Fat Margaret; she would prefer no appellation whatever regarding her basically excessive avoirdupois, though it's hard to miss.) I'm not promising anything, but I mentioned it to that nice Mr. Guccione at the carwash.

Macduff, a somewhat sinewy cat-about-the-house, is convinced of his Druid ancestry. Recently he has taken to scratching pentagrams in the litter box and attempting to call up a kindred spirit from the demon world to help him with his clarinet lessons, which are not coming along as well as either of us had hoped. Night after night we have to listen to rather awkward scales and clumsy arpeggios and every once in a while an attempt at the first movement of Stravinsky's Ebony Concerto, which we were tired of when Woody Herman did it, never mind Benny, never mind Macduff. More recently, he has been sitting atop a stack of old Pete Fountain 78s, which leads us to think that there may be a stylistic about-face in the wind.

Quincy is beginning to carve a name for himself in the business world. (It's "Q loves BH," taking shape in the trunk of one of the garry oaks in the yard.) He has also made some mention of learning to play whist. The four-pawed version is what he prefers, and he would like to learn to play it by himself, since he is unable to come to grips with the concept of partnership play and, anyway, usually exposes one of his backpaw hands by dropping the cards and licking the paw during tense moments of melding in the game.

Big Time Fred, star of the famous Doughnut Party, has been hanging out with the proprietor of an Italian delicatessen in the neighborhood, coming home at all hours, reeking of grappa and munching on prosciutto. He seems keen on obtaining a (small) accordion, and his favorite tune has now become "Kitten on the Keys," although he'd love to get hold of some early Dick Contino albums if anybody has any for sale.

Bradley has won a trip to Reno from the car dealership where he works. His style has been eminently suited to that field of endeavor for a long time, and he moved more Tercels this month than any other salescat. He also sold nine Buick Electras. I mentioned to him who — to say nothing of what — Electra was, and that shook him up not a little, but he is determined to take the Reno trip anyway and asked to borrow my box of silver dollars to take on the chartered DC9. I just hope he doesn't mix his drinks, is all.

So we sit and stare out of the window and strain for the sound of quadripedal footfalls on the flagstones. In the morning, there is — as always — tell-tale evidence: pawprints all over the car, explaining why the footfalls never fell on the flagstones.

The cats continue to get twitchy. It's their role in this life. One of nine.

*T*he Alarming Rise in Pit Cats

---

*U*RBAN TERROR WITH A FUZZY FACE. They lurk in window boxes and past hedges. They hiss crazed kitty invective at anyone foolish enough to venture close. Sure, their fur-some appearance leads people to think they're pettable. But their sharpened fangs, bared in a grimace of terror means you can kiss that one right goodbye!

Their fur is often matted and they sport tattoos. When the fur grows back, the tattoos disappear. They go and get some more. The spinoff industry is Catatoo Parlors. Coke here is the Real Thing. The sound of quarters falling in those machines is a clatter of empty lives, followed after the serious sound of gulping by the sound of empty tins reverberating in life's fulsome gutters.

These are the empties that are beyond redemption.

Were they perhaps bigger they would terrorize the streets on motorcycles. As it is, they drag one another around in small children's wagons, pulled by indentured five-year-olds who seem to have lost the will to resist. The wholesome Fisher-Price logo on the side has been obliterated by ankhs, encircled *A*'s, and other rude signs.

Their graffiti may be minuscule, the words rarely more literate than enraged "Meow Meow" and "Cleo Rules OK," but the message is clear: they are vicious, desperate creatures, disdaining society in favor of the night. Will we take it back from them? Not unless you want a scratch on your arm.

They are the pit cats.

Inspector Wade Made: "We see emergence of new gang activity. Initially it was just the dogs, but now with a recent influx of felines from upper-class neighborhoods, broken, most of them — the homes, not the cats — they move into the inner city. Later, into the suburbs where they find even easier prey."

What sort of prey? Six-year-olds, mostly. Inexperienced posties, new on the walk. Lhasa apsos with identity problems. Toy poodles with their vision not corrected. Arthritic spaniels who couldn't make the transition to the new freedom.

Not for them the jogging whippets or the tough-guy Siamese that remind too much of their own species. No, they go for the weak, the tired, the unwary, the disadvantaged.

What do they want, these modern urban terrors with fuzzy faces? Money? Respect? A seat on city council? Self-rule? Land claim settlements? Mineral rights? More salmon?

"It is hardly that simple," according to Dr. Phyllis Willis, felinologist at the University of Timmins and author of *Purr Deadly: The Heat's on City Cats.* "They are disaffected, angry, confused. They see opulence all around them, but they have no way of getting to it. Their feet are too small to reach the pedals in an XJS. Lacking opposable thumbs — or indeed any kind of thumbs — they cannot count change [apparently dogs with no self-worth left operate the Coke machines for them] or handle money or even credit cards with which to buy microwaves. They lash out, not so much at society or those around them. Their anger is rooted deeper; it is an unfocussed rage expressed at — what? Evolution? The creator? The Way Things Just Happen to be in the Great Scheme of Things?

"They think that being people might be better!"

The most powerful indictment of their desperation finds voice at last. Those who have tried to tell them that being people is no Swiss picnic either have found slim results.

Professor Mick Brick, University of Surfer's Paradise, Australia, has seen them there too, if only in the summer: "I sit on the beach with them, sometimes for hours, getting my head burned [Professor Brick is missing a lot of hair], telling them that humanity is not all it's cracked up to be. Do they listen? No. Do they believe? Not a chance. They're looking for that Big Wave and the trappings that come with it: Styrofoam coolers, pull-tab cans, bad burgers, Coppertone . . ."

They hate Morris, of course, and those effete, long-haired bimbos that get called to dinner by a butler on television.

Their idea of a meal is rat. Still running.

Some people have refused to rent to them. Some neighborhoods have formed vigilante groups that stake out street corners with long green garden hoses and spray nozzles. But it seems somehow too little, too late.

As the inner cities crumble under the onslaught of furry feet echoing through the dark canyons of glass and steel, as the once-safe suburbs succumb to the pathetic sound of furball-coughing in the lonely hours, one thing remains: pit cats are a way of life for those of us who are in the human enclave that is the city.

Maybe it's not quite so bad in The Pas.

Big Time Fred and the Doughnut Party (The First Go-to-Sleep Story for Some Friends' Kids)

───────────❦───────────

*B*IG TIME FRED was round and furry and grumpy-in-the-rain. I don't blame him. Being round meant getting around a lot easier than being, say, flat on one side, or shaped like a truck. It also helped him to roll down hills with the grass whistling past his ears. Being furry meant not having to put on an extra sweater in the winter. And being grumpy-in-the-rain — well, if you're all covered in fur, there isn't much else to do in it.

Big Time Fred had all the things somebody like him should have. A box of marbles, a striped tie for Sunday afternoons in the band shell, a book (in several languages) he didn't read much but kept around to sit on, and a white spot on his nose.

The problem with the spot: people often mistook him for a large, slightly furry snowball, particularly on those nights in winter when he'd come rolling in, a little after midnight, carrying a paper bag filled with doughnuts and his breath smelling just ever so slightly of that very sweet cherry brandy, mumbling something about "late clarinet practice."

Those were all the good things Big Time Fred had, but unfortunately he also had fat feet! Not legs, just feet. They were, to put it another way, fat! Nothing he could do to change that. For a week he went without eating doughnuts (although it made the rest of us pretty upset, Fred muttering to himself all day long, stalking through the place in a temper, nobody being able to read baking books or anything without starting an argument). But it didn't help. The feet stayed fat.

No point in giving up doughnuts in that case, was there?

Another time, Fred painted himself all over with disappearing ink, and although his feet went away by themselves for an hour, every time he put them in the oven or under the sun lamp, there they'd be again — fat.

Now some people think, "Oh sure this is just what you'd expect, isn't it — a fat cat. I mean, it rhymes and everything." But that's not the reason Fred's feet are fat, just because it rhymes with cat. That's far too easy. Blurry rhymes with furry too, and Fred certainly did not have blurry fur. He had fat feet simply because he loved to eat. (That rhymes too, but it's just an accident.)

Most mornings, Big Time Fred would wake up around nine-thirty. He was a late riser because night after night he'd sit up with his big amber eyes staring at the television, where he watched people talk, play the piano, show movies, feed a big black dog some dog food (this wasn't Fred's favorite part, in fact by then he'd usually go into the kitchen for a graham cracker sandwich or something), talk some more, and then all say good-night to each other.

Saying goodnight was the part of the day he liked best. It took him, oh, twenty, thirty minutes sometimes, saying goodnight to everybody, and he had a little list he carried around with him after dark, to make sure he didn't miss anybody.

Then in the mornings, Fred would get up, wash, comb, wash some more, see if there was anything to eat, stand and stretch on a box marked "Whoost" which nobody remembered him bringing home, and then start doing things.

He would sit down at his small desk with the electric windmill and the differently colored jars on it and take the cover off his typewriter. His paws, being fat, would type ERTYUIOP. In fact, ERTYUIOP was one of Big Time Fred's favorite things to say.

"ERTYUIOP," he'd say to the mailman, the breadman, the meter maid, the lawn mower, and the Avon lady. And the doughnut man.

"ERTYUIOP," he would shout out the window, just before going to bed.

"ERTYUIOP!" he'd yell while hurtling down the side of a hill on his toboggan on a snowy baked-salmon-just-before-Christmas kind of day.

And of course we'd all get together every year on his birthday. There we'd all be standing, in front of the house, just behind the tetherberry hedge, and promptly at 4:30 in the afternoon we'd all yell together, "ERTYUIOP!" every year surprising Fred to no end and making him fall out of the hammock.

Luckily for him, though, all the friends knew he fell out of the hammock year after year, and so we always made sure there was a soft foam-rubber mat or a big tub full of whipped cream and jelly right under the hammock, so he wouldn't get hurt. And if there's one thing Fred loved, next to doughnuts and very sweet cherry brandy, it was whipped cream and jelly.

That was his problem, remember. Cream and jelly, doughnuts, garbanzo beans, chopped sirloin, broccoli, french fries, banana cream pie, scrambled eggs, and hot chocolate.

To get back to what we were talking about . . .

What were we talking about, anyway?

Oh yes. One of Big Time Fred's best friends was MGR. MGR was not the abbreviation for manager. Nor was it an acronym for mighty great rumblings. MGR were the initials of Mung Gunga Rao, a friend from Bombay.

Mung Gunga Rao, who looked very much like his name, was a very good friend. Together he and Fred had joined the YCMA

(Young Cats' Mumbling Association), and every June ninth, they'd all get together someplace for the mumbling championships.

What's a mumbling championship? It's sort of like a boat that doesn't talk very loud. But not really. Actually, Mung Gunga Rao can explain it better than I can. But you have to listen very closely because, well, he mumbles.

"Mngh Fjfhg Brzzzz ltltlt bglbgl mmmmmgmgmm."

I thought so.

Together MGR and BTF bought a walloon (a big balloon in the shape of a wall), and on windy days you could see them out near Point Fong, flying it past the peanut vendor and some small people playing down by the grass and tiny sailboats out on the water.

Which brings us to something else that's very important to the story: water. Fred loved it. You see, Fred was originally a Turkish cat. He was a Van cat. In fact in Holland, that's what many people still call him today. Frederic Van Cat (Big Time).

The water was Fred's favorite place on a sunny summer day. He'd stand on the beach, test it with a (fat) foot, look around to make sure everybody noticed his neat new bathing suit, made entirely by himself out of striped things, and then presto! went in, spinning lazily in twenty centimetres of warm water. After that there'd be no stopping him, he went around and around on his back, making circles in the water and eating ice cream with his free (fat) other foot.

This is the factual part: Van cats love being in the water. They're generally white all over. Big Time Fred wasn't, but I did mention that he had a white spot on his nose, didn't I?

Big Time Fred didn't ever play golf. You'd never catch him on a golf course. But he did play Tamble.

Tamble is similar to golf in many ways, except you don't use any golf clubs and there isn't a ball and you don't play it on the grass. Otherwise it's very much the same as golf, except you have to play Tamble on the water with two friends and a small goat named Drindle in a rubber raft, who brings you lemonade and sandwiches, or if you happen to be Big Time Fred, lemonade and doughnuts.

And the nice thing about Tamble is that it's never over. Which means you can never get back to the office once you start a game, which is why no big people ever play Tamble.

You can play Tamble if you like, because you don't have to get back to the office. Mind you, you have to put an ad in the paper to see if there's a goat named Drindle in town. Otherwise it's not much of a game, really (more like golf, actually).

If you want, you can play Tamble for about forty thousand years. Then you can stop for a week, go for a couple of chocolate cream sandwiches and a grapefruit omelette and then get right back to it.

Forty thousand years in the future, here is Fred, still at it. (The grapefruit omelette has been changed to a box of doughnuts, because — well, you know.)

In the background is Mung Gunga Rao and a lady we don't know yet. Actually, I know her, but neither you nor Fred do. Mung Gunga Rao has seen her before, in a bus in North Battleford, but by the time he made his way up front to talk to her, she'd gotten off.

Finally, Fred tired of forty thousand years of playing Tamble. He shook hands with the goat, gave him a nice engraved toaster, and sat down on the other side of the water wishing he had a jar of soap to make some bubbles with. Mung Gunga Rao and the lady from the bus came over to the other side to say hello. The bus lady carried a big box of instruments: trumpets, bagpipes, drums, pianos (very small ones), and guitars. Mung Gunga Rao told Fred that they were all going to a town in Germany called Bremen, to play.

But Big Time Fred, who'd read the book, just like we have, said no we're not, what we're really going to do is open a restaurant and I'm going to make the doughnuts for everybody and you can play the music and wait on tables.

Everybody thought this was a great idea, and so they went to a little island they knew that was looking for a good restaurant (they had seen the sign out some time ago when they went by in a boat, bringing the goat around to play Tamble), and so Fred put on a big white hat which made him look even more like a snowball, and started cooking doughnuts.

Mung Gunga Rao waited on tables. He waited on the one right in the middle of the restaurant for about a week, but nobody came. The bus lady with all the instruments played the harmonium and the trumpet and sometimes parcheesi with Mung Gunga Rao, but still nobody came. And in the meantime, thousands of doughnuts were piling up in the kitchen, because Fred just wouldn't stop making them.

"Have a doughnut!" he'd say first thing in the morning, stuffing himself, and fanning his face with a copy of the menu.

There wasn't a lot on the menu, actually. "Menu," it read. "Doughnuts. Lemonade. Music (9 to 11). Free Delivery." And that was it.

One day Fred and Mung Gunga Rao and the bus lady were all sitting knee-deep in doughnuts, reading the paper, when the telephone rang. Fred answered it.

"We'd like two million doughnuts delivered, please," said someone Fred didn't even know.

Fred got his abacus off the shelf (which Mung Gunga Rao had to work for him because of Fred's fat ERTYUIOP feet — all he could do on the abacus was 111111111) and calculated that there were just enough.

If they delivered two million doughnuts there'd be just enough left tomorrow morning in case any truck drivers came in for doughnuts and chocolate. Not that they ever had in the past, but you never can tell. Word gets around ... So they got the green delivery truck out of the garage and started loading doughnuts into it. When it was full, they drove off. On the way to the place where the doughnut party was going on, Fred whistled to himself.

"Do you think we have enough change if they give us a five-dollar bill?" he asked.

Mung Gunga Rao and the bus lady counted all the change and found they were about eight cents short.

"Maybe we'll get a tip," said the bus lady.

"Maybe we won't," said Mung Gunga Rao.

"You're probably both right," said Fred, trying to be extra-friendly.

Just then they came to the river, and in the darkness (it was night now) they saw that the bridge had walked off the job and gone home to its uncle in Toronto. And on the other side of the river, a big party was going on.

By the magic of leaping across the river in a story we can find out what was happening. It was a jolly party, with lots of people, lots of music and good things. In fact, it was a party that had everything — except doughnuts.

"Where are the doughnuts?" shouted a women, running from room to room. "Where are the doughnuts?"

We all know where the doughnuts are. They're on the other side of the river.

People started coming out of the house and waving across the river and calling to Fred. "Throw them over!"

But Fred couldn't throw very well. He threw three or four, but they landed in the river and floated away. Mung Gunga Rao couldn't throw well either; his ended up in the garden. The bus lady had been a major league pitcher once, but she threw dough-nuts so hard they landed on the roof.

Well, there seemed to be nothing they could do. And the doughnuts were starting to go cold.

Just then Fred remembered something we've all known for a long, long time. His fat feet. And the fact that he loved the water.

"Do you suppose . . .?" he thought.

"Yes!" shouted everybody from the other side of the river.

And so Big Time Fred picked up the doughnuts — about half of them, actually; he could always come back for more — and tested the water with a (fat) foot.

His fat feet worked just perfectly, like pontoons or snowshoes or water-wings. If he walked ever so slowly, sort of shuffling as though he had big slippers on, he could make it across, but he had to balance very carefully with a million doughnuts in his hands.

When he got to the other side, everybody shouted and clapped him on the back and somebody finally remembered to throw a large rope across so Mung Gunga Rao and the bus lady could climb over and join them.

And the party — which was just about the best party anybody has ever been to — went on till all hours.

I was waiting up, about four o'clock, I guess, typing this story, when there was a scratch on the front door.

It was Big Time Fred. Grinning a little, carrying a bag full of doughnuts, his breath smelling ever so slightly of the very sweet cherry brandy he loved.

"Have a nice time?" I asked.

"ERTYUIOP," he said and went straight up to bed.

He was probably right.

*S*phinx and Cheops and Ted and Alice and Puss and Boots

———————— ❧ ————————

*P*LENTY OF PEOPLE are into pyramids. Most of them are dead now, of course, but there's been a revival; something about the power of pyramids to stop, if not reverse, ageing, keep lawn mowers sharp forever, focus brainpower, putting razor blades and knives in so they'll cut like — razorblades and knives.

Some people have a little pool-triangle of mandarin oranges piled under a pyramid and still fresh from way before the war. Some have taken to sleeping in pyramids, asserting that it lets them get by on a lot less downtime and wakes them up all refreshed.

Trader Vic — the original one — kept wines for his San Francisco restaurant in a pyramid cellar. Don't know whether he wanted to slow down ageing or speed it up. Either way, the wines had a separate page on the list and cost more.

I read not long ago that some pyramid-prone people have found that their pets enjoy sleeping in pyramids. They wake up more alert, able to play the trombone after only two or three lessons, and walking about the house reciting Longfellow. Is this what we want from our pets? I decided to try the theory for myself. And my furbucket friends.

I built a lovely pyramid out of mahogany, carefully checked all the specs and drawings, and put it in the middle of the living room. I sprinkled a little Hanselian trail of catnip to the entrance, as an extra enticement, and set up a whole Muybridgean battery of sequentially firing cameras with little trip wires so I could document the experiment for *Scientific American*, and waited.

Or maybe it was Gretelian. The trail of catnip.

Nothing happened for a long time. The cats regarded it as a funny thing with a point on it. Dumb décor. It wasn't edible. It didn't run off when poked at, and it was difficult to sit on top of.

After about a week, one of the cats decided to go inside the pyramid and go to sleep. This happened at three-fifteen in the morning. The tiny creature's foot-pressure on the sensitive plate inside the pyramid woke me at once, and I fell down the stairs in my rush to witness the memorable moment. The startled cat immediately left the pyramid and went into exile under the sofa.

Some weeks later, the cat attempted the pyramid once more. This time I was ready. Soothing the cat with a slow song from *Eugene Onegin* — aren't they all? — I soon caused him to fall asleep.

A few hours later, I reached in to see how he was doing. Imagine my surprise when I cut myself on his fur!

I now have the sharpest cat for six blocks, solid proof that pyramids really do work. I have managed to get as many as twelve shaves off a single cat without having to put him into the pyramid for recharging. Not only that but he can now open his own tin of Miss Mew simply by sitting on it and rotating 360 degrees. There is a lot to this stuff, I'm telling you. Don't just dismiss it out of hand. And be careful petting strange cats.

C*at Recipes of Sorts (By and For)*

———————❦———————

CHOCOLATE MOUSE (not to be confused with Chocolate Mousse, or, for that matter, Chocolate Moose, a particularly Canadian dish, impossible to prepare without a support group.) [See Moosing Bees: Social Interaction in the Kitchens of Early Canada (Hurtig)].

Ask your butcher to butterfly one mouse.

Find out why your butcher has suddenly cut off your credit and no longer gives you one of those cute calendars at Christmas.

Coat mouse with chocolate syrup. Arrange on bed of lettuce, rapini, and very thin slices of sole.

Call cat in from badminton. Explain concept of "chocolate" to cat. Leave the room and let cat eat Chocolate Mouse in peace.

In the morning, when discovering uneaten Chocolate Mouse atop your $200 facsimile edition of the complete Salman Rushdie novels, take Chocolate Mouse, place in washed cat food tin, pretend to put lid back on tin. At dinner time, make a great fuss pretending to open it, simulating can-opener noises or whatever turns cat on.

Offer imitation-tinned Chocolate Mouse to cat again.

Bribe neighbour to borrow budgie. Give budgie 1/32 Valium. When budgie is relaxed, place it on cat's forepaw (tie forepaws first to avoid possibility of unneighborly row). Call friend who rf Cat Recipes of Sorts (By and For)

works for local tabloid and get photo taken for Sunday Lifestyle section filler. Take money received from newspaper (first make sure they are prepared to pay for cute, exclusive photograph) and buy bottle of Lagavulin sixteen-year-old malt whisky for butcher, explaining momentary lapse of sanity, and attempt to get credit privileges back.

Feed cat liver and bacon, a couple of raw eggs, some fresh shrimp, and half a bottle of chilled Chablis.

Drink rest of Chablis and wonder at marvels of nature.

POPCORN BALLS WITH CATNIP

Pop plenty of corn in usual manner. Do not salt, but pour lots of melted butter on. Add some kind of nontoxic binding agent to hold kernels together after poppage is done. Roll in fresh-snipped catnip (dry will do if it's from around Arnprior). Form in balls, squares, parallelograms, or, if ambitious, replica of *Spruce Goose.*

Try to interest cat in popcorn ball (-square, -gram, -Goose). (Cat will roll it about the floor, pounce on it, to a lot of typical cat behaviour, anything except eat it.)

See if dog is interested.

Kids?

The postie . . . bridge club members . . . maybe Uncle William . . . *any*body?

Didn't think so.

ALICE B. YOU-KNOW-WHO H*** BROWNIES FOR CATS

Find telephone number of girl you went to first-year college with, the one with all the Gerry Mulligan albums who was always reading Kierkegaard and saying the name wrong.

Make long-distance call to Anchorage, where she married

forest ranger in '68. Apologize for getting her out of bed at 2:30 a.m. Ask how the kids are: Oh yeah? Yeah, me too, oh you know, still writing, trying to lose some weight; no, we split up years ago . . .

Ask if she can remember recipe for those brownies with the you-know-what in them (getting all twitchy like in the old days, in case the line's tapped).

Prepare brownies as per directions, substituting catnip for you-know-what, chocolate, flour, sugar etc. Bake revolting-looking green mixture until cats are attacking oven with catapults and things.

Serve, while averting eyes as customarily dignified cats make total fools of themselves.

(Another nice dish is Broccoli and Cauliflower Surprise: fresh, raw cauliflower and broccoli, in bite-sized chunks, drenched in a vinaigrette of olive oil, red wine vinegar, lemon juice, black pepper, salt, dry mustard, and tarragon, all acting as a suspension for four or five lightly bruised garlic cloves. The surprise aspect, as you have guessed, is that kitty is not the slightest bit interested. Well, it's hardly surprising, is it, but it is an observation on the nature of things.)

❧

Sparrow in Phyllo Pastry: Prize-Winning Recipe by Foggy, Former Barn-Cat

(Foggy is a former barn-cat in Maple Ridge, British Columbia. The mother of 32 kittens, she taught herself to cook early on, between litters, on a Coleman camp-rig. While professing a strong preference for domesticated birds, she laughingly admits that trying to wrestle a chicken — plucked or otherwise — into a square of thin dough is beyond her physical capabilities. She has found that robins or sparrows are best. This new recipe continues in a tradition of exploring the world's cuisines that began with last year's winning recipe, Foggy wins a two-week holiday in Costa Rica with Kenny Rogers. (The other one, not the singer!).)

This recipe serves six.

6 sparrows, plucked and not too badly mauled, cleaned
   (reserve liver if you can find it)

package of phyllo pastry	1/2 cup finely chopped onion
melted butter (unsalted)	oregano, thyme, black pepper
feta cheese, crumbled	6 slices bacon
olive oil	2 medium tomatoes, seeded
3 hard boiled eggs, diced	and juice squeezed out, dice
1/2 cup finely chopped	celery stalks, onion studded with
carrots	2 cloves, bay leaf, parsley
	(for boiling birds)

boil birds in water with celery, studded onion, bay leaf and
  parsley for about 8 minutes

drain and dry

leave birds whole or section into fourths

unroll phyllo pastry to maximum dimensions

depending on size of squares, layer 2, 4, or 6 leaves for bottom
  of sheet

put bottom layer on oiled baking sheet

sprinkle layer with chopped carrots and onions

drizzle melted butter on top

add layer(s) of phyllo, drizzling with salt and pepper, thyme
  and oregano

chop bacon and sprinkle on birds

more phyllo

next layer: tomatoes and hard-boiled eggs

more phyllo

next layer: feta cheese

finish with phyllo layer (double or triple ply)

drizzle melted butter on top, sprinkle with pepper

have oven at 375
put phyllo-creation into oven for approximately 35 minutes
let cool slightly, slice into individual squares for serving

Serve with: leaf spinach, sauteed or steamed beans with pink peppercorns and caraway. Wine: 74 Beaulieu Vineyards Cabernet Sauvignon or Mateus.

Nights of Ennui:
21 Bedtime Stories for Insomniacats (Index Only)

"*T*ELL ME A STORY, then," said the cat, wide awake as always, not even a nictitating membrane so much as a-flutter. It was past two o'clock, an hour when decent folk and their felines are asleep. But not here.

This had been going on for months now: sleep all day, watch a little prime-time television, maraud your face off, stroll in fine as you please, sit in front of the fire and damn near fry. Ever notice how they all seem to do that? Lie there, dangerously close to the fireplace, getting so hot the fur almost ignites, but will they move an inch? Sooner get the fire department in here.

Then, just about the time I figure it's safe to tiptoe away up the stairs — he's asleep, he's asleep! — I stumble on the catnip mouse, fall back down only to land right in front of the fire, and guess whose — or what's! — eyes I'm looking into?

Now, I am just as capable of telling sleepy-time stories as the guy who's heading up the credit union investigations you invited to the Soroptimist luncheon. But cats don't just want *a* story, they want a special sort of story: intrigue, intellectual stimulation, something to challenge the alleged mind, a few philosophical observations rooted less in reality than in tuna.

And so, the Twenty-one Nights began. That is how long it took me to get the cat to fall asleep. Not quite so long as Scheherazade, no, but then there wasn't quite as much at stake either — although by Day Fourteen or so I figured there was.

These, then, are those stories. Or at least their titles.

And when Number Twenty-one concluded with the fabled Danish storyteller getting his invitation after all, was there the sound of merry snorage? In your hat, as the Xingu! say, only in their own dialect.

"That's the most boring thing I ever heard," said the cat, stretching.

"Well, it was supposed to put you to sleep, stupid." I was getting a tad defensive. There wasn't a lot of air in here either. "Did that, all right," said the cat, "Goodnight."

Out like a light. I moved the screen in front of the fireplace. No point trying to move the cat. There's a kind of special glue they secrete that melds the fur into the fibres of the carpet when they're sleeping; miraculously, it evaporates on awakening.

It was a new moon out there. It was the Hour of the Wolf, as Ingmar Bergman called it, the hour before dawn.

What the hell did he know? It was the Hour of the Cat Asleep at Last.

And I was wide awake.

The tales themselves? Ah, that's another story. But here are their titles. There's some soporificity in those alone.

1. Kid Galvanized
2. How Stuttgart Exploded
3. The Trombone Fire
4. Mixed Vegetable and Brandy
5. The Gerbil Symphony
6. The Football Game That Everybody Won
7. The Penguin Lesson
8. Hurricane Clancey

The twenty-one stories in full? That's another book.

Visiting: A Go-to-Sleep Story for Some Friends' Kids

———❦———

*T*HE DAY THE FIRST LEAF fell down the cat sat on the porch and watched it go.

"I suppose," said the cat, "it means the pheasant will be back soon." And the cat sighed and strolled the length of the leftover flower bed, looking for a warm shaft of sun to roll the afternoon away in.

The cat was right.

In the morning, just before it got light, before the newspapers hit the porch where he usually sat and before the early workers slowly drove down the street, scraping the windows on their cars, the pheasant peered over the hill.

He looked fine. The summer in the back part of the ravine, where the blackberries were and the ferns, had filled him out a little and now he was waiting for the winter.

He remembered the cat, a little. And he was a bit nervous.

The cat sat inside the house on a window ledge and blinked an eye. He yawned until his face seemed to be all mouth, but he wasn't sleepy. He was wondering.

120

"He's gotten bigger still," said the cat to himself, looking at the pheasant. "There'll be no chasing him anymore."

The next day, they met.

Accidentally, in the back. The cat had gone up over the hill, to find out why the leaves there were making so much noise, falling. The pheasant was a little bit asleep in the sun. When he heard the cat coming, he scrunched down in the leaves and tried to blend in. The cat smelled the pheasant, a little too late, and fell over him.

A little hiss, a little arched back, a little flap and flutter and a startled noise. Then, a few feet apart, they settled down to stare at each other.

"It's you," said the cat finally.

The pheasant nodded his head up and down.

"You've . . . put on a little weight."

"So have you," said the pheasant as he looked the cat over carefully in case he'd missed something.

"But," he checked, "still no feathers."

The cat smiled a little.

"How is the other side of the ravine?"

"Very nice," said the pheasant. "You should come some time. Blueberries, blackberries, some wild strawberries, sunflower seeds, lots of things. How has the summer been here?"

"Quiet," said the cat. "Some visitors, an argument or two. A brush fire." The cat looked up into the branches of the scraggly oak trees. "The crows fierce as always . . ."

Slowly, the cat and the pheasant edged closer together as they talked.

A field mouse scurried by beside them.

"Have you had lunch?" asked the cat.

"Oh yes," said the pheasant. "I ate earlier. There's a little bit of seed left." He indicated a small pile. The cat shook his head, no thanks.

When the sun went behind the hill and it quickly grew cooler, the cat knew it was time to go back into the house. Soon his people would be home. They'd open tins and pour milk and chop meat and scrape vegetables in the sink. He had a difficult time telling which was which, and sometimes they fooled him, tossing a bit of broccoli or a piece of onion as he'd scramble after it. Oh well, it made them happy, thought the cat.

"I'll be here tomorrow, if you're not doing anything else," said the pheasant.

"I might see you then," said the cat, and brushed himself off.

The pheasant watched him angle off across the big lawns.

In a moment, the door of the house opened, a yellow box of light, and let him in.

The pheasant thought it might be foggy later, and fluffed his feathers.

That night the first frost of fall came. With it came a startling sound.

The pheasant woke under his log. Even the cat woke up in his house.

"Geese," said the pheasant to himself. "Flying away again."

"Noise," said the cat to himself. "I'll see it in the morning if it's worth seeing."

The cat brought a newspaper out to the hill the next morning. Since neither he nor the pheasant could read, the two spent a pleasant hour ripping it up and climbing under it.

The startling sound came again.

"Did you hear that noise?"

"Geese," said the pheasant. "There will be more. Don't you remember them from last year?"

"No," said the cat. "Last year there was a dog. It's all I can remember, about last year."

That afternoon, a flock of geese went by overhead and they watched them go.

"Why do they do that?" asked the cat.

"I think they have a place they go to, where it's warmer."

They heard a distant dog worrying about someone walking by.

"And maybe with no dogs," muttered the cat, as his eyes closed a little, in the warm sunshine.

"It's very comfortable here," said the pheasant on a patch of moss.

One afternoon, they found a pile of windblown leaves, against the base of a rock. They were standing on top of the rock, looking out over a very small valley.

"This could be a good place . . ." the pheasant began.

The cat licked his mouth a little nervously. Then he looked up for reassurance, but there weren't any geese that day. Then he looked down again at the leaves, and finally, he looked at the pheasant.

"Well, let's try that."

First the pheasant, and then, immediately after, the cat. They jumped off the rock.

Neither of them flew. The cat plummeted, but landed on his feet. The pheasant flapped and fluttered and his wings worked like a parachute.

The cat hurt his pride and the pheasant bruised a wing tip.

"I can fly, a little," said the pheasant. "But mostly for emergencies. Is it true that you always land on your feet when you fall?"

The cat was miffed.

"I wasn't falling. I was flying. No it isn't true. And in emergencies . . ." he pouted, "I snarl!"

"That won't help you get off the ground," said the pheasant.

The cat turned his back and walked towards the house.

"Don't be angry," the pheasant called after him. "I can't snarl. The geese can't either."

The cat didn't look back.

That night, when the people were drowsing in front of the fire, sipping their wine, the cat managed to knock a book about flying from the shelf. During the night, he looked at the pictures.

None of it helped.

The pheasant was up early. He watched the cat ambling towards him, whistling to himself.

"Nice morning," said the pheasant.

The cat nodded. "I wasn't angry, yesterday. I was just . . . sort of sad."

"I know," said the pheasant. "You get like that when it's autumn. Everybody does."

In the afternoon, they heard a flock of geese going over the hill.

"There they go again," mumbled the pheasant, half asleep.

"Have you ever talked to one of them?" asked the cat.

"No. What would I say?"

"What is it like . . . flying?" answered the cat. "That's what I would say."

"It's nice," mumbled the pheasant.

Both of them were startled when they heard a wingflap noise nearby. "You stay here," said the cat to the pheasant. "In case it's dangerous."

"But it's a bird of some kind," said the pheasant. "You stay here and I'll go."

They both went.

Together they crept up a little ledge and peered over the top.

A goose was sitting on the rock, looking at the little pile of seeds the pheasant had left. Beside it was a bunch of shredded newspaper from another morning.

The pheasant made a polite little cough.

"Good afternoon."

The goose turned around and looked at them. When she saw the cat, she backed away.

"No, no. It's quite all right. The cat is a friend," said the pheasant.

The cat had backed away, too, as the goose flapped her big wings.

The cat and the goose sat on opposite sides of the ravine, the pheasant between them.

"Would you like some of these seeds?" asked the pheasant.

The goose said nothing for a moment. Then she pecked at some of the sunflower seeds.

"I think I got lost," she said after a while.

"How can you get lost?" scoffed the cat. "You can fly, you can see everything up there . . ."

"Sometimes you get lost," said the goose.

"Where are you going?" asked the pheasant.

"South."

"What's south?" asked the cat.

"The place where the sunshine is. And all the food. And all the other geese."

"I think I'd sooner be by myself," grumbled the cat. "You fliers have a nice afternoon, then."

The cat stomped off across the lawn.

"He doesn't seem very happy," said the goose.

"He gets like that," the pheasant told her. "He wants to fly."

"Oh," said the goose. "I wonder why."

The two birds picked at some seeds and spent a fine afternoon together.

It rained in the morning.

The cat sat on the window, grumbling about the rain and looking out at the hill. He saw the pheasant and the goose standing on top of a rock looking at the house. The cat thought he saw the pheasant give a little wave of a wing.

"They're getting all wet up there," he thought. "Why don't they find a log to sit under?"

It rained for a few more days.

The cat hardly ever went out in the rain. If at all, it was usually for only a minute or two. He'd look around, sniff the air, make sure it was still raining and then dash back in.

Around lunch time one day, the cat was sitting in the window, when he heard a scraping at the door. He sat bolt upright and crept to his door. Standing outside on the porch was the pheasant. A little ways off, down one of the steps, stood the goose. The pheasant looked up at the door handle. The goose looked nervously across the lawn.

"I can't open the door," called the cat. "What do you want? It's raining. You'll get all wet."

"I was wondering if you were all right," called the pheasant.

"Of course I am."

"I thought perhaps you were angry."

"About what?" asked the cat.

"About my friend, the goose. About the fact we can fly and you can't."

"Oh I don't care about that," said the cat.

"Then why don't you come out to see us anymore?"

"Because it's been raining. I'll see you when it isn't raining anymore."

The cat wanted to wave at the pheasant.

He leapt back up on the windowsill and looked out as the pheasant slowly turned from the door and walked towards where the goose was standing.

"He doesn't like the rain," said the pheasant to the goose as the two of them trudged across the wet lawn and up the hill.

"But he's not angry."

The cat tapped the window, but they didn't hear him.

"I'm not angry," said the cat. "I don't have to fly. I'm quite happy being a cat. A cat who has a pheasant and a goose for friends. Now that's something."

He watched them go.

"Be careful," he said after them. "You'll get wet."

The sun came out the next day and as soon as the door was opened, the cat bounded out and up the hill. He ran right up to where the goose and the pheasant were. The pheasant laughed, and the goose, who was still not used to the cat, fluttered her wings.

"What have you been doing?" asked the pheasant.

"Sleeping, mostly," replied the cat.

"Well, we're going to sit around all day," said the goose.

"Me too," said the cat and settled in beside them.

It was very warm and the ground steamed a little bit.

The cat thought it reminded him of a sauna but the goose and pheasant didn't know what he was talking about.

Actually, neither did the cat.

One morning, it was frosty again, with the trees and leaves edged in white and crunchy.

"It's getting time to go," said the goose to her friends.

"I thought you were lost," said the cat.

"Well, I know which direction to go, so I'll just go and keep on going until I meet some friends. But thank you for the visit. Maybe I'll be back in the spring."

She walked over to the rock which the cat and the pheasant had jumped from once. She flapped her wings, once or twice. The cat and the pheasant waved.

The goose lifted off and circled them once.

"Have a warm winter," she called to them.

The pheasant waved and waved.

"Don't get wet," said the cat.

The next morning, it was all white. Snow had fallen.

The cat made his way very slowly through the snow, leaving footprints where he went.

Up on the hill, the pheasant was waiting.

"Goodbye," said the pheasant. I stand out in this, so I have to go. It's time to move farther back into the trees."

"Goodbye," said the cat. "I think it's time for spending most of my time inside now. Well, see you in the spring, before you wander off to the ravine for the summer."

The pheasant slowly walked into the trees, knocking snow from the branches. The cat ambled off back down the hill, leaving marks in the fresh snow, while the pheasant trekked into the trees.

Overhead, the geese went by, very high and very fast.

And left no marks at all.

Their long sound seemed to hang in the air after everyone had gone.

The winter was here.

PART THREE

Jogging with Beethoven

From Ailurophones to the Kitchen Zink

❦

*T*HE HISTORY OF MUSICAL INSTRUMENTS is very old indeed, predating even the GST and Lucite-heeled shoes. After the Dark Ages were lit up and the common folk could see their way about a little better, music enjoyed a great burst of activity, popularity, unsolicited credit cards, and other indicators of affluence. There was music in the churches, music at the courts, music in the streets, and sometimes even music behind the house. There were troubadours, trouvères, and *trous de normand*. There were meistersingers, minnesingers, schlechtensingers, and a lot of people who couldn't make the Kiwanis Music Festival finals in Hamburg. There was music in the air, and musical instruments putting it there. But where are all those old instruments now?

Museums of original instruments abound. The Brussels Museum of Musical Instruments is justly famous, and the Dolmetsch Collection one of the most comprehensive, yet many people have ignored some of the other establishments that serve as repositories of ancient instruments.

The East Holdham Museum of Genuine Old Things, for instance, has several decommissioned ailurophones in its collection. These curious instruments were fashioned from clusters of dried and minced garlic, to which were added two and a half cups

131

of chopped onion, a little olive oil, a dash of salt, and ground pepper to taste. Not capable of producing sound, ailurophones were nonetheless a very tasty dressing for zucchini and other squashes. (They are not to be confused with aelurophones, which were nothing more than basic bugles with the shape and sound of a cat!)

Also worth mentioning is the Kanemaker Collection of String. Although the collection in itself isn't remarkably musical, careful scholars will be able to see how much of the string displayed here could have been (and indeed was) used to make sounds somewhere in the musty pages of antiquity.

There is also the East Tarkus Drive-In Musical Instrument Museum and Casino, just off Highway 19 in Nevada. I haven't visited it myself, but it has a favorable review in the *Nevada Tourist Guide*.

Scholarship has played a major role in the preservation of valuable ancient instruments. Countless scholars have written on the subject. Among the lesser known is Achtbesser, the German explorer and inventor of the canary, whose *Die Musik und andere Komische Sachen* is, if not one of the most lucid collections of notes, certainly one of the most voluminous. Sir Bernard Whistlepin's historically inaccurate *Musical Expression and Depression* has been purchased for film production, under the working title of *Knights in Bondage*, and promises to be controversial if nothing else. Finally, D'Acapo's *Historia Musica Ipso Facto* stands out as one of the most inconsequential books of his or any other time. (D'Acapo, incidentally, is more famous as the man who invented the portable cassette tape recorder in 1709, but was forced to abandon the project because he could not persuade any of his contemporaries to invent electricity. A prototype steam-powered cassette recorder proved far too unwieldy: on a trial run from London to Cornwall, it took out several bridges along the road, damaging crops and injuring scores of townspeople who'd crowded the King's highway to jeer and point.)

Musical historians such as Achtbesser, Whistlepin, and

D'Acapo (not to be confused with the famous vaudeville team of the same name) have documented the rise and fall of numerous instruments.

Throughout the bumpy roller-coaster ride that is musical history as we know it (or, indeed, as anyone knows it) many instruments had a brief, meteoric rise and fall. Maybe money played more than a small part in that. I wouldn't know.

Among these we find the terpodion, a friction instrument invented in Berlin where, of course, a lot of that sort of thing was going on. We have also the flexatone and the musical saw, both of which are still in some use today, despite considerable efforts to have them banned.

Benjamin Franklin is credited with inventing the glass harmonica. How and why make if not fascinating reading then at least something to fill the time until your train comes.

As usual, that evening (a Monday, I think) Franklin had left his wallet in the car. He was having dinner at a friend's restaurant, still there after the place had officially closed, and since the automobile had not yet been invented, the friend saw through the flimsy trick at once and banished Benjamin to the kitchen to help Rodrigo wash up.

Around two o'clock in the morning, having the place to himself, Franklin lined up a row of wine glasses, dipped his finger in the Palmolive (which explains history's fascination with his very smooth hands), and proceeded to rub the rims of the glasses. After cutting his finger a couple of times on a few that shouldn't be used for serving anymore, anyway, he gave that up and went home to discover electricity. If only someone had been at work on the telephone at the same time, Franklin thought, he could have called up D'Acapo and history would really have gone for a flyer! These things happen all the time, in retrospect. Also in Europe.

There was another instrument, the philomela, which is self-explanatory, I think.

The zink was one of those odd instruments that was particularly loathed by Henri Kling. In the score of his "Kitchen Symphony" (*v.* Raymond Lewenthal's recording, Angel), the composer specifically forbade any use of the instrument. We read, in the autograph: "For all and any kind of domestic instruments, save the [kitchen] zink." The brackets are my own, as is the umbrella in the hall-stand.

The buccina was a Roman army horn used to signal the changing of the night-watch. It had a dragon's head painted on it. Rambunctious musicians, during frenzied public concerts, would often smash the instruments against their amplifiers to the delight of fans and also the Genoan Buccina-Works, *s.a.*

The ophicleide is the largest key-bugle ever devised. It measures some thirty-one metres and stands more than two storeys tall. Only two were built, and both of them are still standing; having been joined by colored walkways, they now form part of the Pompidou Centre in Paris. I think that's just fine.

The Aida trumpet was an interesting instrument. Essentially, it consisted of your ordinary 1.3 metres of drawn brass tubing in a loop, making a B-flat trumpet. However, *Grove* tells us, "For Aida, on stage, in the second act, it's made straightened and pitched in B-sharp." The process of straightening and pitching caused no end of confusion in the pit during the Act 1 interval, as a man with an oxyacetylene torch made his way through the brass section. He was known as the Aidatrompetenmeisterschweisser, and may still be.

This instrument reflects Verdi's not inconsiderable egomusiccentricity — I mean, asking certain instruments to be modified simply for one act of one opera! What happened to the trumpets *after* Act 2? Were they bent back? And imagine what would happen if every composer specified such self-indulgence: in *Madama Butterfly* we'd have the pinkerton fiddle (or Suzuki violin); the La Sonnambula oboe (or sleep clarinet) would come to be, as well as the Menotti medium-rare bass. It just makes one dizzy.

The hecklephone was invented by a disgruntled concertgoer who wanted to be able to make his displeasure known more loudly during certain sections of some of the lengthier Bruckner symphonies. Actually, Strauss takes the blame for the introduction of the instrument; no less a work than *Salome* specified it during the 1905 première.

Finally, there were the kits, and though they've left home now (one is in dentistry, another in the civil service, Bitsy's still "finding herself" in Manitoba), they're worth remembering. These eighteenth-century precursors of the Suzuki violin were very tiny fiddles, so small they could be carried about in a shirt pocket. They were synonymous with the crwths and much easier to pronounce.

Many instruments gave rise to fascinating ancillary development. In the flute group, consisting of pan pipes, bladder pipes, reed pipes, and gemshorns, shepherds did much of the designing and experimenting. All right, *some* goatherds did too.

The original instruments of this family were short lengths of cane with fingerholes, upon which these country stalwarts spent much of their time playing simple tunes. So much time that they neglected their flocks now and then, causing many sheep (and some better-educated goats) to simply wander off the edge of the earth, which was still flat at that time.

Bladder pipes and bagpipes were also prominent among these rustics, who had good access to the natural materials required in the instruments' construction. Bird keepers found it much more difficult to devise pipes that sounded: the ill-fated Albanian featherpipe represented a monumental effort by some designers, but the thing simply couldn't be kept in tune or made to sustain more than the briefest of tunes because of the immediate escape of air.

It is said of the Emperor Nero that he "knew how to play the pipe with his mouth and the bag thrust under his arm." Fair enough, but what of the all but forgotten Emperor Dymaxius, who knew how to pat the top of his head with one hand and at the same time rub his stomach with the other? Not so musical, you say. But were you *there*?

The gemshorn was a natural animal horn, and here again attempts had been made to use other portions of the animal. Pigs' feet were tried in some of the Silesian villages (e.g.: das fusshorn or, as it was known in Leipzig, das schuhorn), and an unsuccessful instrument made from dried sheeps' ears, known only in Germany as ohrtrompete, can be listed among those deserving of failure.

To the extant transverse flute and straight flute, we must surely add the numismatic obverse flute, the reverse flute, and the mystical perverse flute, often played during satanic rituals.

Among early keyboards we find the portative organ, the renaissance organ, and the positive organ. But what of the negative organ — a devilishly tricky instrument that would simply not make any sound whatsoever, causing most of the music written for it to be dismissed in the score simply as "tacit"?

Among the brass we find older instruments such as the clarion, the buisine, the slide trumpet, and the serpent. Originally, trumpets were made of wood, later of brass, and a brief attempt to fashion them of leather proved virtually pointless.

The serpent is aptly named. It originated in the Garden of Eden (near Yemen), where Adam and Eve were sporting. One day, during some pleasant sport, God came wandering down the path, and Adam, quick to size up the situation, grabbed a snake from out of a tree they'd been sporting under and, in order to silence the animal, stuck an apple into its mouth.

"What are you guys doing?" asked God in that brusque and direct way of His.

"Just playing the serpent," said Adam. "Anything you'd like to hear?"

"Yes," replied God, "I'd like to hear how come the serpent has that apple stuck in its mouth, is what I'd like to hear. I thought I told you not to pick them while they were green."

God waited.

"Aw God," said Adam, squirming. "It's sort of like a harmon mute, and . . ."

But God had turned and walked back to the summerhouse, and that meant only one thing: get out and get a job.

In the woodwind group over the years we've found the racket and the curtal, the cornamuse and the kortholt and the rausch-pfeife. This last is German and some believe the name derives from *rusch* (meaning rusch), which evolved simply into "reed pipe." The true meaning comes from the German for opium (*Rauschgift*) and for pipe (*Pfeife*), and it means "to smoke until you become silly, but it's all right if you're De Quincy or Wilkie Collins."

The curtal is considered an embryonic version of the bassoon. The nineteenth-century musicologist Ritter von Taschentuch in his book *Curtailing the Curtal* suggests it be banished from the ranks of the orchestra or at least made to sit perfectly still until 8:30 (9:00 Newfoundland).

Also of German origin was the racket (although anybody who's ever been on the Algeciras-Tangiers car ferry will attest other-wise), which was a long-handled thing flaring into a flat oval, across which were strung lots of little wires. Sound was produced by causing the instrument to come into contact with a ball (German: *Ball*) propelled by a smart flip of the wrist. This may be blatant untruth or pure conjecture; old pictures of people playing the racket show it to have the appearance of a small Thermos bottle into one end of which the players blew. The sound was pretty much the same.

The cornamuse should not be confused with the French word for bagpipes (*pipes du bag*). The oldest written description of the instrument can be found in Praetorius. The kortholt is quite similar but was spelled with more *k*'s and *t*'s.

Of the strings, interesting relics are the theorbo, chittarone, cittern, ceterone, orpharion and the tromba marina — a small trombone anchored in Bremen Harbor to which boats could pull up and get ice.

The theorbo was larger than the lyre (but it was also older), and the chittarone larger still, until we reach the cumbersome maxima monumentarone, taking up the space of the "sixe horseys and a manne to guyde themme," as Chaucer writes in "The Tale of the Miller's Wife and the Horrendous Fork."

Three instruments in this family have not survived at all: the penorcon, poliphant, and stump, named after a medieval law firm near Bristol. They made poor music but apparently distinguished themselves in corporate law and were later knighted. The subsequent Sir Penorcon, Sir Poliphant, and Sir Stump were not heard from again until the second act of *A Midsummer Night's Dream*, believing the making of music to be better suited to the lower class and contenting themselves with drinking a good deal of port after dinner until they had to be carried up the stairs and put to bed.

Instruments of which nothing at all is known any longer include the whipsnade, the falernum, the alto custodian, the semblance, the zucchini-organ, the obtacle, and the hang-dog. We can only imagine . . .

Neusidler's hunerg'schrei was a large stuffed chicken that was bowed with a palm frond; the mysterious ftangg was revived only once or twice in this century, and that's ample.

Though most of these instruments have mercifully disappeared, one question remains: What of the music they made, the compositions that required their playing? The answer is concise — Shaw puts it nicely when he says, as Corno di Bassetto: "What does it matter, now?"

Perhaps the oddest and least frequently heard instrument of all time is Switzerland's fabled Lake Fehler. A small alpine lake lying in a valley between the cantons of Mschwindel and Gstagstn, it is known to sound only once every forty-six years, when the moon is in the ascendant, Venus is in the outer house, and Mars and Saturn have passed out cold on the rec-room floor. Musicologists describe it as sounding a bit like a distant truck crossing the Iowa state line pursued by a malamute with a head cold.

Most composers have given up even trying to write for it. These people weren't born yesterday, you know.

Moving Modern Opera Smack Dab in the Middle of All That Theory You Learned

———————— ❦ ————————

VOLTAIRE, IN A SOMEWHAT Dorothy Parker mood, once said of the opera: "It is nothing but a public gathering place, where we assemble on certain days without precisely knowing why."

Of course, many of us know exactly why we've assembled. We just couldn't get tickets to the hockey game. During a moment of corporate magnanimity, we pledged a year's support to the South Central Saskatchewan Opera Group, and now it would look foolish to pull out and put the money into renovating the Lloydminster Plant. One of the kids is in the chorus. What's more, everybody who's anybody is there.

But since those days of quippery by Voltaire, opera as a form of art and entertainment has fallen on hard times. Oh sure, the Seattle Opera has its Wagner Hotline and its Norns sing in English, while posters show mammoth mamas mia with platefuls of spaghetti announcing that the opera is so good "you'll eat it up." And the Vancouver Opera Association once mounted an inspired advertising campaign with the zippy slogan, "Relate to

Opera!" which was obviously devised by an advertising agency whose previous account was heavy machinery. And the Met's still making music with the aid of Texaco and cute but incomprehensible quizzes in the middle; Bayreuth's got bombast, the Canadian Opera Company is selling with sex, and occasionally we get to see something by Britten on the tube, with "Cheers!" preempted yet again. But is it enough?

More to the point, is it really *communicating* with Mr.-and-Mrs.-and-Ms.-and-the twins' everyday reality, RV in the driveway, Big Mac attacks, and all. Does opera still manage to focus the parabolic antenna of its vast Verdiesque radio telescope directly into the gas-cloud nebulae of just plain folksitude, or is it all just bad prose?

Quite apparently the problem centres around the subject matter of present-day operas. Opera subjects may be, according to *Grove*, "Tragic, comic, heroic, allegorical, spectacular, legendary . . . anything suitable to dramatic treatment." But what about lifestyle? What about the Feifferisms, the Koren, the Hamilton, the Johnny Hart, for that matter? The real, one-on-one, meaningful personal interface, that kind of performing opera? Can we tell where it is coming from? Will we be able to predict where it is going? And, perhaps most important, will we be there when it gets back?

Those are the questions that must concern us as we consider singers who sing to attain superstardom, though nothing like Paula Abdul. We regard make up and costumery so cunning as to make an ageing diva appear as a sixteen-year-old Albanian shepherd with a speech problem, though nothing as elaborate as Ace Frehly. We hum along with catchy little tunes (though I confess that if I hear "Mi chiamano Mimi" once more before the turn of the century, constant listener will simply fwow up!), but, let's be honest about it, nothing as memorable as "More Than a Woman."

And we digest the words of writers who prattle, usually during midafternoon programs on network radio, about operatic performances, in terms best characterized by "Beachcomber's

Roland Milk": "This infinitesimal noblesse of Machina's inter-pretation of Talamodo, the scarcely sentient fisherwoman is tantamount to a type of deliquescent triumph over avuncularity. Here too, a supposition of latency comes into play, giving way to forced-air heating and splendid brio, though some of the colors were missing from the box." That sort of thing.

Perhaps it's due to isolation, self-imposed in Monroe-doctrin-ish half edicts issuing from under furrowed brows of otherwise sensible weekly newspaper columnists. Today, with commercial breaks every six minutes, phone-marts, and Beaujolais in pouches, people quite simply won't sit around for rehashed tired stories or edgy philosophical riddles set to music. We need more, new, and better.

The great Giuseppe himself may have been on to something when he wrote in a letter to his pal Antonio Somma: "I would be willing to set even a newspaper or a letter to music, but in the theatre the public will stand for anything except boredom." Somma sent him the Sunday edition of *Le Figaro* (he kept the crossword for himself) and nine months later, *Tosca* was born, both father and daughter doing fine.

Some things some relatively famous folk said on the subject: Mr. Gluck? "I endeavored to reduce music to its proper function, that of seconding poetry by enforcing the expression of the sentiment and the interest of the situation without interrupting the action or weakening it by superfluous ornament." Having made that statement and not even sorry, the somewhat pedantic operatic reformer appended to it his greatest superfluous orna-ment, *Alceste*.

Herr Wagner? "Everything lives and lasts by the inner neces-sity of its being, by its own nature's need." Already, we can see that Wagner's job writing birthday card verses was going to come to an abrupt end and he would be spending the balance of his life making ponderous art.

David Randolph reminds us that "*Parsifal* is the kind of opera

142

that starts at six o'clock. After it has been going for three hours you look at your watch and it says 6:20."

And Delius, interviewed in the early part of this century, foresaw the fact that brevity was once again becoming if not wit then certainly where the money was, when he said of the future of opera: "Length and cumbrousness will be first to disappear . . . opera will look to brevity and conciseness; short, strong emotional impressions, a series of terse scenes." Doubtless he hadn't evisaged anything quite so terse as the work of Lukas Foss, who has written an opera that lasts just eight minutes!

It may well have been Foss whose work also signalled something of a turn in modern opera when he set to music Twain's story of the jumping frog contest in Calaveros County. Is it any sillier than *La Fanciulla del West*?

There's simply not enough good swashbuckling left, for one thing. Maybe James Bond or Modesty Blaise might make for good operas. Maybe we have to find a new source of love stories; there can be no more remakes of *Romeo and Juliet*. Perhaps all those Harlequin romances can serve as source material.

Perhaps the bestseller list, although quickly turned to celluloid, might yield some subject matter. No one has done anything with Arthur Hailey's works yet. *Airport* may be tough to stage, though there's lots of good staging technology we can borrow from Wieland Wagner. Think of the other possibilities. Montserrat Caballé in *Fear of Flying*. Sherrill Milnes and Joan Sutherland in *Looking for Mr. Goodbar*. Galina Vishnevskaya and Nicolai Gedda in *The Whole Earth Catalog*.

Also, our major authors should be contributing their talents to opera by providing good libretti and adaptations of some of their own works, instead of sitting around in writers union meetings and vowing to help some of those unfortunates who are still struggling under the weight of their first Canada Council grant.

Why isn't Pierre Berton in there, for example? To the best of my knowledge he hasn't published a thing this week. *Choo-Choo* could become a darling little work, staple of endless outdoor festivals. Farley Mowat could contribute an opera about wolves, though if he chose whales he'd probably get more support. Colombo could do one that takes the whole weekend, with singers appearing in shifts, and using as its text all the quotes he has collected by Canadians on the subject of apple danish.

The composer Menotti says that any subject is suitable for opera "if the composer feels it so intensely he must sing it out." Well and good. The man who gave us *The Consul* and *The Medium* and *The Telephone* is reputedly working on *The Cuisinart*!

Legend and native lore, mythology and the classics, they are all rapidly drying wells for operatic waters. But there are endless new possibilities to be considered.

Pornopera may well become popular; *Candystriped Stewardess Nurses at Club Med* is bound to be a hit. Or what of science-fiction opera? After all, consider the amazing success of such *soi-disant* SF as *Star Wars* and *Battlestar Galactica*. Add a good score, trim the lines by 90 percent and dress the singers in aluminum foil, and off we go with *Revenge of the Grape People* or *Dr. Azimuth's Amazing Proton-Smasher* or *Meech Lake*.

There's a motherlode of rich material in real life. I have one Pavarotti might like; it's called *Edge of Afternoon*:

Bert (tenor) comes home one night from the Agency (baritone) to find his wife (soprano) has left the budgie on. There's a note (B-flat), which he sings. It tells us nothing. The TV is on and there are some sparks out back near the garage (bass). In the second act, he falls over the refrigerator. "Damn these small fridges," he sings again and again. Later the telephone rings. It is a wrong number (alto). Finally, the neighbor comes over to borrow a Butterball turkey and a cup of Lafite. They make love. Bert's wife comes home, singing "It's all a mistake, this is supposed to be a surprise party for your birthday!" and there are all of Bert's friends (tenors), the priest, and that nice Mrs. Gallagher from the credit union looking on disgustedly as he tries to pull his pants on. Bert's mortification is endless (contralto). In the final act, he has locked himself in the root cellar. It is February, but he is still alive. The village priest, Father Martin (speaking role), comes up the path, convinced he is in the wrong opera. There is a thunderstorm, and Bert's wife finds peace at last with a couple of novels by Margaret Atwood. Their nine-year-old son, Spirit Mountain, Jr., has dropped out of his rolfing lessons. Bert finally comes out, an old, broken man, really sorry for being a jerk — and who should be waiting for him with open arms at 125 at f5.6? A photographer for the *Daily Dart* and a cub reporter. The epilogue shows Bert clutching the paper, with a screaming headline (coloraturas): "Idiot comes out of root cellar after 18 years. Thought he was hunted by Ethiopian agents." Reading the story, and finding his name misspelled, Bert falls over just as the house next door is being subdivided.

Now *that's* real. I think it might well be the sort of thing Pavarotti's been looking for, as a vehicle for a television special out of Montreux or a lounge opener for his MGM Grand act at Las Vegas.

Opera can, if properly planned, scheduled later at night, and preceded by a special announcement, provide us with a good vehicle for blood and gore. Now that television is no longer a safe repository for basically hostile emotions all of us harbor, opera may become the place for it, without fear of jeopardizing the impressionable psyches of our children. They're not going to want to come along to four hours of opera when they can stay at home and watch "Starsky and Hutch" with the babysitter!

The type of meaningful, in-depth reporting that characterizes such publications as the *National Enquirer* will lend itself magnificently to the new operas. *Giant Killer Bees Invade Dry Cleaning Plant*: sounds like the sort of opera Ned Rorem might write. Perhaps he will. Or *Jujubes Touted as Cancer Cure and Mothproofing Substance. Can Donny and Marie Ever Find Happiness or Is the Elusive Quality of Life Basically an Intangible Denied These Two*

Cutie-Pies? Maybe that's a little too long a title to get on the label without obliterating the little dog logo, but you know what I mean.

But I think the best would be a Hugh Johnsonesque opera: a dark, robust, perfumed work with a long nose and bouquet that fills the Western Hemisphere, called *Tall Goblets*. It is the story of a magnificent Beaune, the Nicolas Rollin cuvée, and how it begins as ripening grapes on the slopes, how it makes its way, pressed, into Beaune, how it rests in a big cask in the cellar, under Hospices, and a lot of Belgian buyers spit on it one mid-November. How it gets bought at the auction by a bunch of guys wearing "Team Beaujolais" jackets. How it is racked and clarified, bottled and shipped around the world until finally, in the closing scene, no one and nothing on stage but the bottle as it faces the end . . . or is it the beginning? The cork is pulled and slowly the lights go down as the bouquet fills the hall.

Do you think we could get Beverly Sills to reconsider, for that one?

Debating da Bagno

───────────── ❧ ─────────────

*C*OULD ANY HUMAN BEING really write such music? History proffers only muteness when we question it closely on the subject of Vasca da Bagno, the "Mystery Man of Milano." While scholars readily shout the secrets of other composers to the uncaring ears of an ever-burgeoning bunch of musical snoops, there is only a small pause mark on the staff where da Bagno's life lies written in a cramped hand and 6/8 time. But da Bagno wrote more than six hundred concertos in D for flute during the spring of 1709 alone! We also know that he ran an orphanage and that he was very fond of those little Polish plums in chocolate.

Though he played no instrument, he is said to have listened with such fierce concentration that the critics and writers of his day believed he had made a pact with the devil to listen "better than any man alive." Some biographers have written that he often booked music halls, sold tickets at outrageous prices, and enticed a goodly number of Milanese to come and watch him listen. Other critics have pointed out that these people actually went only to listen to the string orchestra and paid little attention to the red-bearded idiot in the carpet slippers sitting stage-left with his eyes shut. It's the eternal conundrum of "who you gonna believe?"

Da Bagno's official biographer, a largely illiterate sculptor named Caviglia, tells us that the composer was first born in 1681 and then again in 1690, both times near Naples. His father was a council wrangler; his mother freelanced as a travel agent for the Medici family. Into this carefree, upper-middle-class, culture-bereft environment came the young Vasca. He was left on the da Bagnos' doorstep early one Christmas morning by the Sisters of Indecision, a not-so-charitable order based in Reykjavik.

From an early age, the lad's musical talents were duly noted and reviled. There were no instruments in the da Bagno home — save for some of the forceps, biceps and sextants da Bagno *père* required in his work — but there was a good, full cutlery drawer. In only a few months the youngster was busy banging forks and knives about, and sometimes cutting his chubby little fingers. Caviglia says that the Concerto for Fork and Continuo (C.688), which dates from this period, is one of da Bagno's greatest compositions. But that's precisely the kind of blinkered and pig-headed thinking we have come to expect from narrow-minded musicological wonks like him.

At the age of eleven, Vasca da Bagno was thrown out of this jolly family tableau when he refused to stop banging his Beatrix Potter bunny-cup on the table. Finding himself on the street with nothing more than a bunny-cup and the clothes on his back, da Bagno thought that he might well end up in an orphanage. There was, as yet, no thought of running such an establishment. But fortune intervened in the form of a bored young political science student, and part-time prince, who took da Bagno into his home for six or seven years. Some numbskull scholars assert that this was actually sixty or seventy years, but I find it impossible to believe that anybody could put up with da Bagno's incessant cup-banging for so long — no matter how strong the initial attraction may have been.

As for the events of the period, history (and even Caviglia) are discreetly silent. Suffice it to say that although there may well have been music made, there sure as hell wasn't any written down! The only memorable incident was the ricotta episode, which occurred a few years after the meeting between da Bagno and the prince.

One day — I think it was in February — the prince asked da Bagno to go to the store for a couple of tubs of ricotta. Da Bagno never returned. The prince took out small-space classified ads and had a lot of little posters plastered in cafés and Roman baths and bus stations. But he never saw his friend again. Nor, we're told, did anyone else. Da Bagno had mysteriously and effectively disappeared, just as if he had simply walked off the edge of the earth.

It wasn't until 1751 that he was discovered again, hanging precariously by his fingertips from the underside of a little fishing village in Portugal. Sure enough, the fool had walked off the edge of the earth. But the kindly ministrations of some Portuguese anchovy fishermen helped him back up. They dried him off and fed him some delicious clam broth. Da Bagno gradually grew to love Portugal. He developed a strong affection for these simple folk, and the little papyrus boats they used, and some of the soulful music they sang (a kind of Douro River delta blues then called *falar*), and especially some of the jolly rich, dark red wine they would quaff in great quantities. He found it a great deal better than the watery Valpolicella he'd become used to. And so he decided to stay a while.

Setting himself up as a soothsayer (to overcome the fact that he spoke nothing of the language), he told fortunes by examining the sediment in port bottles. This gave him a rosy outlook, slurred speech, and, in due course, gout.

Awakening one morning in the gutter, just outside the Norwegian embassy in Lisbon, da Bagno knew that he had reached the bottom. He attacked a passing bank clerk, robbed him of two and a half million escudos, rented the top floor of the Tivoli Hotel, and called up room service. All day long he ordered the things he needed: a piano, some pen and ink, a metronome, a music tutor, several models willing to pose nude, frozen dinners to last till the weekend, and some new short-sleeved shirts with penguins on the pockets.

Here began da Bagno's most creative period, lasting for seven days. During that intense week, he composed nine Christmas oratorios; 108 symphonies; seven song cycles on Amalia Rodriguez songs; another six hundred concertos for flute, this time in B-flat, making them fairly difficult; a really dreadful string quartet called "Intimate Letters, A to C"; sixty-two operas based on Shakespearean plot summaries from a bootleg copy of *Lamb's Tales* he had found in a hotel night-table; and more that three hundred sonatas for the autoclave. But it wasn't until he was in the taxi (one of those creaky old Mercedes diesels) on his way to the airport that he realized his true calling was to write tone poems. Thus, lurching through the streets of Lisbon and on the subsequent TAP flight to Milan, he not only pioneered this form but wrote the book on it. In a few short hours he composed close to seventeen thousand such pieces. Some were, of necessity, short and unsuccessful. But others, notably "The Ashtray," "Young People at the General Delivery Wicket," "My Foot," and "The Dog's Breakfast," are cherished items of the standard repertoire.

Back in Milan, da Bagno went underground again. Some scholars claim to have seen him near the sewer outfall at the edge of the city, but that was likely just Gabrieli.

When next Vasca da Bagno surfaced in the pages of history, he left a large black stain. Having been appointed organist to the court of Duke Polvere (a blatant piece of favoritism, since da Bagno couldn't play a note), he proceeded to embezzle a large sum from Povero Polvere. On his way down the fire escape with a load of lire, he was apprehended by the sleepwalking duke and challenged to a duel. Da Bagno drew his sword, and the duke (who had seen this kind of artwork before) shot at him. He missed, but the shot woke up the household. Da Bagno was cornered. Standing on the fire escape wearing a foolish little half mask, carrying a lot of money, and surrounded by faithful retainers to Polvere, da Bagno realized that there was only one way to escape his predicament. He had to buy his way out.

Beginning with Polvere's old father, Hugh the Taller, he pressed handfuls of bank notes into the pockets of the faithful. By the time he reached the front door, he had given the doorman, the footman, the noseman, and the Irish setter several million lire apiece. He thus found himself outside the palace but without any money whatsoever. He had given away not only his entire recently acquired fortune but also his parking change, his lucky fiver, and his Visa card — which didn't expire for another eight months.

In disgust, Vasca da Bagno shot himself in the head.

It is perhaps indicative of the calibre not only of the pistol but also of da Bagno's overall aptitude that he missed, even at this close range. When the dust settled, he was sitting on the cobblestones, a little dizzy, but otherwise unhurt. He slipped into a nearby rare books store and disappeared among the pages of history once again.

Da Bagno's music has been totally and justifiably ignored. Hanslick confessed "irrational revulsion" for it, while Avison found "nothing remotely Handelian in any of this." The Abbé Vogler felt da Bagno "didn't exist," and Addison spoke of his sixty-two operas as "poor variations on the same theme." Perhaps most pointed in his criticism was Calvocoressi, who stated outright: "If you so much as use my name in this piece, you're looking down the wrong end of a lawsuit." It was a clumsy mix of metaphors, but Calvocoressi left his intentions crystal clear.

Of recordings of da Bagno's music, the less said, the better. The London (Ontario) Records package of the complete symphonies, with Dorati and the Philharmonia Hungarica, is perhaps definitive, for no one else has even so much as recorded one da Bagno symphony. Some years ago, there was a pressing of Sir Thomas Beecham in rehearsal, working his way through the second movement (Adagio slitta con spreco voce) of da Bagno's

Forty-fourth Symphony in D, C-sharp minor, and F, subtitled "The Inconclusive." But the disc was quickly deleted because of some of the abusive language that came from the cello section. An attempt was made to record one of da Bagno's Christmas oratorios (*Amahl and the Pannetone*) at Spoleto one year, but due to a strike by electrical engineers, the event was mercifully averted. The song cycles haven't been touched by anyone. There was a Vox Box of the autoclave sonatas some years ago — in fact, this was the largest Vox Box ever, numbering 112 discs and packaged in a shipping crate. The now forgotten soloist from a Midwestern medical school received a good review in *High Fidelity*: "Ambitious musicianship, concerted effort . . . just to lift it . . . a definite . . . something . . . to be . . . heard . . . if not . . . or, who?"

Rumors have it that the Juilliard Quartet digs out the score of da Bagno's only string quartet at their annual New Year's gathering and plays it for friends, laughing gleefully all the while. But this is only conjecture. The more than twelve hundred flute concertos have, of course, all been recorded. The first twenty measures of each concerto are available on a sixty-five-disc sampler set called "Les moments, n'est-ce pas, magnifiques de Rampal?"

Vasca da Bagno died quietly in his sleep in the autumn of 1768, and again, during a tug-of-war contest across the Saône, in the summer of 1774. What he was doing in France at the time, nobody knows. At his funeral, Albinoni's Adagio was played at twice its normal tempo (it had started to rain), and the eulogy was delivered by his longtime childhood friend and mentor, the former political student and part-time prince. He praised da Bagno's ability to "disappear on an errand so simple as getting some blasted cheese" and urged those assembled to "forget this fool as quickly as you can, there's true talent waiting in the wings."

Some scholars argue that the prince's decision to use that moment to introduce his latest protégé, Lima da Unghie, was a bit tacky. In any event, it was really starting to come down now, so everybody wept. The "Mystery Man of Milano" had gone to his last reward. It is reputed to have been 27 lire for "working with orphans, however briefly" and a stern admonition from one St. Peter to "stoop banging that silly bunny-cup up and down!" But here again, history proffers muteness. And rightly so.

*M*usical Maverick Gets Big Bang
Out of Life

❧

SHE'S NEAT, SHE'S FUN, she's fashionable! What's more, she's got more talent in her left arm than most people have in their entire lumbar region. She's on to "real" yogurt, into videotape rolfing, lives with her Afghan hound, Big Bill Gurdjieff, and has a Bloomingdale's charge card that she's never used but carries for ID.

She is, in short, what classical music was all about in these slapdash, whiplash eighties, and she may well spill over some of that enthusiasm, through the magic of CBC Transcription recordings, into the elegant "we're-out-to-be-your-lifestyle" nineties. And beyond that decade?

"Why worry about it?" bubbles Susannah "Susannah" Tellbright, timpanist with the Fort Chippewyan Symphony. Our titan on the timps is bright, vivacious, fun to be with, and she *certainly* knows her music.

Citing Carl Palmer and Ginger Baker among her early influences, she soon realized that these sources weren't "cool" (as she puts it in her own off-the-cuff manner, a style of speaking strongly redolent of an easy promiscuity with the English language and not dissimilar to that of a former lady in these true northern parts).

154

Pretty quick on the uptake, the downbeat, and the draw, Susannah "Susannah" soon began citing James Blades and William Kraft, not to mention Christoph Caskel and Max Neuhaus.

"Mind you," she recalls easily, "Caskel was pretty tough to cite!" And then the laugh, and she's off again on another round of speaking engagements, Rotary Club luncheons, bad cheque charges, and visual recollections.

Timpani was the farthest thing from her mind, at the beginning.

"I couldn't even spell it," Susannah "Susannah" smiles, sipping another of her ever-present tins of Diet Beaujolais. (She's hardly had a day without the drink since her first time in Paris, when she studied with Boulanger.) ("No, no, no!" she corrects me emphatically. "Small *b*. Not the musicologist. I was taking an advanced brioche course at the Cordon Bleu. Or maybe it was the Sorbonne, I can't remember. You know that building with the leaded windows . . . ?")

First she went to work in a travel agency. But there was a longing, a necessity for self-expression, and banging the drums seemed somehow to "fit the bill . . . or is it foot the bill?

"But you know," she reminisces easily with strangers, a problem that generally keeps her away from New York City, to Bloomingdale's dismay, "in Fort Chippewyan you don't just head down to the Co-op and get a set of timps. And it's pretty tough too to find somebody to teach you the ropes . . . or is it the sticks?"

Her first local teacher was Sergei Ulachuk, drum major with the Fort Chippewyan Police Pipe Band and Volunteer Fire Brigade. She has since studied extensively with the National Research Council Official Time Signal ("Timing is so critical when you're a timpanist . . . or is it a timpaneer?") and later in Paris with Chuck Delancey, a cabaret drummer for many years whose father had once known Milhaud's grocer.

It was in that wonderful city's active musical bonhomie (or is it boheminenne?) that she met Messiaen, but he was with another woman at the time, so our fledgling percussionist didn't get the chance to talk to him. "Still, there was an unmistakable presence about him," remembers Susannah "Susannah."

She has recently premièred Steve Reich's lengthy percussion piece "Drumming," transcribed for solo timpani (or is it timpanum?) in Fort Chippewyan Moose Hall, for an appreciative capacity audience consisting of her parents, Bill and Eleanor, and the relief teacher, but she had to abandon the project when the lease ran out on the building and the work was only about a third played.

Active in community work (Blue Cross, Green Shield, the Hospital Auxiliary, Welcome Wagon Hostess, and a paper route), as well as having been featured on recordings (she sang harmony for her brother Ernest's punk-band, Hatemail, when they did a demo for Eleanor Sniderman, which was not returned — setting them back about fifteen bucks each, by the way!), her real ambition is to be "on CBC Radio every evening, sort of like Shelagh Rogers. I think a steady job would be terrific; you don't have to worry about anything except getting along with nine producers, six writers, fourteen technicians and about four hundred freelancers. That's my kind of work." she says with a sigh.

She has been asked to perform this summer at the CBC's Dead Air Festival in The Pas, and she's a frequent guest lecturer for the Saskatchewan School District No. 49 Adult Education program, covering such diverse topics as nursing, Albanian dialects, coppertooling, and yoga for the chronically disinterested.

Is there a lot of work for a timpanist in Fort Chippewyan?

"You bet!" says Susannah "Susannah," adjusting her gimlet. (She has switched to the hard stuff midway through our discussion. It is summer by now, and we are on the porch of the cabin, in our swimming gear.) "But not much of it musical!"

Why the double name, I ask her next.

"It just sort of happened," she says smiling. "I think it has a little to do with the song about the banjo, or else it's from Greek mythology. My father knows."

A common sight in the Safeway parking lot with her specially designed diesel Rabbit with it bubble dome on the back to accommodate her instruments, Susannah "Susannah" has her sights fixed firmly on the future.

"My horoscope says next Thursday is good for Geminis."

Her being born in April doesn't worry her. "There's bound to be spillover . . ."

Some of the world's major composers are writing for her. Elwood Lortzing, the renowned electronic music composer and weapons expert from Uranium City, has created a special work for her called "Some Stuff, for Timpani and SaskaTel." In performance, Susannah "Susannah" dials a long-distance telephone number chosen at random, and when the overseas operator answers, the musician gives her timps a good sharp whack while holding the mouthpiece over the membrane. The results are taped and sent to Stockhausen.

She also thinks Hans Werner Henze may be in the process of writing a solo work for her. "He called a couple of weeks ago, and even though I wasn't home, my mom spoke to him for quite a while."

From here, it's all downhill for our lady of kettledrums, and we can expect her first CBC solo album within the decade. Or maybe the next. She's cautiously excited about it.

"It's too bad they tell you what you have to play. We're doing the Mozart No. 21 Piano Concerto, the Overture to *Abu Hassan*, and a piece for six flutes and string quartet by Harry Freedman (or is it Bruce Mather?). It's going to be tough to get a real feel for that kind of music on the timpani."

Because my car was stolen from the driveway, I ask if I can spend the weekend.

"It's too bad '90 Minutes Live' isn't on TV anymore," she muses, oblivious to my question and nervously fingering her Bloomingdale's card. "I'd have been a perfect guest for Gzowski."

Well, she may have something there.

It's a good thing for Canada she's not about to part with it.

Jogging with Beethoven

AT A QUARTER TO SIX in the morning the telephone rang.

"Ah, *perfido!*" muttered the missus as she rolled over and pulled one of the pillows from under my head. I struggled to light a candle. "It's that bloody Beethoven again."

It was.

"Only the flint of a man's mind can strike fire in music," Ludwig chuckled into the receiver. "But I can run like the wind. Or something like that. Let's go."

I pulled on my blue running shoes with the yellow stripes, grabbed a scarf, and laced my trousers. "Don't come back to bed all puffing and freezing," said the light of my life. "If you're going running, at least get some breakfast into you."

"Not running, dear — jogging," I muttered. "With Beethoven."

"Well, I suppose it's better than sitting up all night playing poker." She was asleep again, and I was already out the door and off to meet the great composer.

Most musicologists have ignored the fact that Beethoven was a fanatical jogger. Indeed, it was our mutual concern for physical fitness that caused us to meet in the first place. I'd stopped at the mailbox by the Methodist Chapel and was watching kids toss the folded *Vienna Angenehme Zeitung* onto porches. Frankly, I was out of breath from going only a couple of blocks.

As I stood there, who should come around the corner by Haubenstock's Konditorei but Beethoven — in a smart track suit, a little too small for him, his Adidas pumping the pavement, he all the while whistling at top volume and puffing like a calliope. I recognized him right off from the plaster bust my piano teacher had in his living room.

"Hi," I said. "How's it going?"

"Tough, but it keeps you young," he said, and he was off again, narrowly dodging a *Zeitung* destined for Haubenstock's porch.

We met on many a morning after that. He was usually ready to stop and chat, all the while running on the spot. I was usually out of breath — shameful, really, since he was twice my age.

"Have you read Schiller's column this morning?" he asked me one day. "*Seit umschlungen Millionen*, indeed. Next thing, he'll have us all unionized." Ludwig laughed and chugged up the block.

I thought to myself that morning, as I stopped to tie my shoelace: if only future generations could see the composer of the magnificent Fifth, puffing up Geistliche Strasse in a slightly small, red-and-white track suit with white piping up the legs.

Never mind generations. If only Alexander Thayer could see him! But Thayer was probably still asleep, someplace in Massachusetts.

One morning Beethoven was running late.

"Lots to do today, people coming over, letters to write. Do you remember how 'The Bear Went Over the Mountain' goes?"

I hummed a couple of bars.

"Great, perfect, just the thing. It's going into 'The Victory.' Would you mind dropping this in the mailbox for me on your way?" And he handed me a big manila envelope addressed to Bettina von Arnim. I was tempted to take it home and steam it open, but in the end integrity prevailed. I just dropped it into the little blue-and-yellow box and hoped Thurn and Taxis wasn't going out on strike. Then I headed home to oatmeal and sachertorte.

It wasn't long after we'd become acquainted that Beethoven started bringing sheet music with him on those mornings he thought we might meet on the corner. "A little something I whipped off last night. Thought you might like to glance at it," he'd mutter offhandedly and thrust a sheaf of manuscript at me.

"What is it this time?" my good wife would ask, when I'd lug it all home.

"Another symphony."

"Well, put it in the shed, with the rest. You can't move in this house for falling over allegrettos anymore."

It was in this way that I got to see much of the master's music that hasn't survived the years. During one summer, Beethoven penned a composition for the Commonwealth of Australia (on a bet) called "Adelaide," and another in tribute to a British tuba player, called "Oh, Hoffnung" (opus 198). The same summer he dashed off twelve German dances, five variations of "Rule Britannia," fifty-seven Irish songs, and one nasty letter to his cousin Charles, who owed him money. There was also the sprightly Andante con molto sfogliano of "Annoyance," which he dedicated to his landlord.

He claimed to enjoy composing while jogging. I suppose that accounts for the style of some of the later quartets. Certainly it serves to explain the Grosse Fugue.

When a commission came from a union local of sheet metal workers in Saarbrücken, it must have been his landlord's stubbornness that caused him to accept the job. Certainly, "Die Blechschneidermusik" caused him endless frustration. Indeed, he never completed the work.

Though he dashed off "Wellington's Victory" in a matter of days, it took him most of the following autumn to compose "The Defeat of Alf Johnson" — a musical chronicle about a poker-playing friend who'd lost a huge split-pot. It had been commissioned by the Kiwanis Club for a roast planned for Johnson on the Sunday after Labour Day.

The bagatelles were fun. Although today we remember best "Für Elise," there was an endless string of these dedications: "Für Frau Leistenhaupt," "Für Harvey," "Für Uncle Des," "Für the Second Avenue El," and so on.

Beethoven acquired a cairn terrier named Faithfu' Johnnie. The rarely performed "Für Faithfu'" was his tribute to the dog, which died of ennui after hearing his master rework the second movement of the Kreutzer eighteen times in one weekend.

One day Beethoven inherited some bagpipes, and on autumn mornings you could hear him practising his pibroch. The instrument became an obsession with him. Originally, the Choral Fantasia was scored for the pipes instead of piano, orchestra, and choir. Although a certain Angus von Frimmel wanted to première it, Beethoven couldn't arrange a performance in Vienna. Finally, he restructured the whole thing, not without some difficulty. "It doesn't sound Scottish anymore," he muttered when I met him backstage after the première. "But they seem to like it."

Beethoven was a great one for entertaining.

"We're having a Christmas party," I told him one day. "Feel like dropping over and playing some carols on the piano?"

That night, a little after nine, Beethoven arrived — with his bagpipes! By midnight, after we'd sung our throats raw on "The Campbells are Coming" and "An die Ferne Geliebte" and "Unten, bei dem Alten Mühlenstrom" and "Ode to Billie Joe," nobody cared.

Beethoven tipped back his glass of Siebenzwergenthaler Spätlese, stood up, and stuffed the bagpipes into his carrying case.

"Need a lift home?" I asked him at the door. "Rasumovsky's going that way, soon as we can wake him up."

"No, thanks," said Beethoven. "I think I'll just jog."

He slipped on his Adidas, stuffed his ruffled shirt into his track pants, and dashed off down the road, Faithfu' Johnnie at his heels. My wife and I were standing in the doorway, watching Beethoven and the dog disappear into the fog.

"That man," said my wife, "is going to catch his death of cold one day. All that running! Help me get the count on his feet and let's go to bed."

I slowly closed the door against the winter night, but not before the cat crept in on little fog feet. "Where have *you* been?" I asked, not really expecting an answer.

"Chasing that fool cairn terrier with the Scottish name, running down the street after the greatest composer of our time," said the cat. "Is there any lox left?"

I pointed into the rumpus room. "Unless Rasumovsky ate it all."

One by one, the candles went out all over Vienna. I opened the bedroom window to let in some air. In the distance I thought I could hear fast, receding footfalls, accompanied by faint whistling I recognized at once as being the theme of the Eroica. And, every once in a while, the faint wheeze of bagpipes. But I could have been mistaken.

Time to hit the hay.

At a quarter to six on Boxing Day morning, the telephone rang. "Ah, *perfido*!" said the missus.

Concert Etiquette

───────────❦───────────

THERE'S A CERTAIN ETIQUETTE for almost everything from cricket matches to state dinners, annual meetings to barge christenings, golf tournaments to legal separations for people who've decided to be adult about this whole thing. A lot of people live by those rules of behavior.

So why, then, should it be that the same people who wouldn't say "boo" during a crucial putt, and who always know instinctively which fork is used to approach the quenelles, can't seem to get through the performance of a piano sonata without a major physical crisis?

The worst of it is, they always end up sitting one row behind me at the concert, a couple of seats too far left so that I can't casually drape my arm across the chairback of the masked lady at my side and smash the offender's knee with the swizzle stick I stole from the Fours Seasons Garden Lounge. The noise-makers usually bring their knitting or they spend quite a lot of time at what sounds like tearing the shrink wrap from the complete Wagner Ring Cycle, disc by disc.

I suppose it must seem quaint to some people, but I go to a concert to hear the music most of the time. The people around me have usually come to discuss that MacArthur woman and she with those two cute little girls barely into kindergarten, or to

count the number of Gucci bags in the audience or the number
of wales in a foot of corduroy or any one of a number of things
not necessarily related to listening. (I once sat in a perfectly
splendid cathedral listening to a Schubert Mass, while a man
across the aisle from me wound his wristwatch for what seemed
like forty minutes. I was tempted to trade him my self-winding
one, but he probably would have waved his arm up and down to
activate the mechanism.)

Of course, concert hall lighting doesn't help matters any. The
people beside you are always leafing furiously through the program to see if this is the part that's symbolic of the fjord or
heralding the entrance of the comedians in a wheelbarrow.

There are some "activities" that occur during concerts that we
should discuss. If we can define and isolate the symptoms, make
people understand that they are not alone, and provide some
sensible working solutions, perhaps it will help us achieve the
one thing I'm prepared to pay double for next time I'm at the
concert: silence from everywhere except the stage.

Having to Answer the Call of Nature: Well, this one is unavoid-
able, of course. But it is a good idea to look at the program in
advance. If the movements of the piano concerto are to be played
without a break, govern yourself accordingly — most of them run
the thirty-to forty-minute range. If Gustav Mahler's Symphony
No. 2 is on the program, it might be a good idea to pass up the
concert entirely; it could be agonizing.

*Having Consumed a Whole Bottle of Veuve Clicquot before the Concert
in the Little Russian Restaurant She Likes So Much*: A toughie, this
can give rise to what is indelicately called belching and which can
sound even more indelicate in the doing thereof, especially
coming unheralded about twelve bars into the Adagio (or Quiet
Part). To avoid embarrassment, you may wish to suddenly look
about near your feet and feign having dropped something of
value. A more drastic solution is to drink only still wine before
the concert, although this may mean having to worry about No.
1, above.

Being on a Diet: This occasions the rumbling-tum syndrome, and it often hits at the point when the guitarist and the conductor are exchanging meaningful glances to make sure they're both playing the same Vivaldi concerto. About the only solution is to ask your companion if you might borrow her mink and pile it on your midriff as a muffle for the duration.

Rustling around in Your Seat to See if Bernie and Eleanor are Here: It's a good idea to accomplish this maneuver before the concert actually starts, if you can. If, as is usually the case, Bernie and Eleanor tend towards tardiness you can take my word for it — they're here and yes, they would love to join you for a drink after.

Bringing a Transistor Radio to Catch the Hockey Scores: Unless there is music by Karlheinz Stockhausen on the program, this can cause friction with your neighbors. If, of course, you have five dollars riding on the game, you might be forgiven, but you're still faced with the problem of trying to find a break in the music to explain your predicament to those around you. Those little earplugs are useful though. A word of warning: remember that the cord runs down from your ear, across your arm, and into your lap. Don't suddenly leap up to join the standing ovation, or the radio will clatter to the floor. Nobody will hear it, but you'll end up at Radio Shack in the morning shopping for a new one.

Humming Along to Parts You Know: When you wear one of the above-mentioned earplugs, this is a nice, friendly way of letting people know you're no stranger to Havergal Brian's Seventh Symphony, or that the soloist has nothing on you, but it can be distracting to those who don't know the work but would like to, which is why they came in the first place. Those of you with a key to the office after hours can photocopy the score in advance and bring along copies to pass around, so that everybody can follow along. Humming can be forgiven if you're Keith Jarrett or Oscar Peterson (and you should wear one of those "Hello, my name is" stickers on your lapel), but just about everybody else should really be dissuaded from making this a habit.

Tapping Your Foot to the Rhythm: This behavior is a natural outgrowth of playing along with the drum solo in a nightclub, using your swizzle stick on the rims of glasses and ashtrays. If you find that tapping is an uncontrollable act, foam-soled shoes might help.

Waving at the Percussionist You Once Met at a Party: There is nothing innately wrong with this maneuver except that it may cause the French horn player to think you're waving at her, in which case she could lose her place and the Konzertstück would crumble right then and there. Then the conductor would get upset and there'd be a scene after in the dressing room and, well, you know the kind of bad feeling this sort of thing can generate among artists, sensitive lot that they are.

Brushing Your Hair: In the dark this tends to create sparks. The gesture may be acceptable in some of the shorter works of Charles Ives, but hardly anybody plays these anymore. Ask your companion to pat it in place for your under the pretence of having him help you off with your coat.

Unwrapping Boiled Sweets: Try to limit yourself to four or five and space them so the unwrapping can take place during the applause. If you're not sure when that's due, keep your eye on the conductor. If he puts the little stick down, a tentative clap or two to "sound things out" may be in order. If he has left the stage, you're fairly safe (unless there's music by Mauricio Kagel on the program). If you're all alone in the hall, go ahead, unwrap a pound. Apropos sweets, crackling your MacIntosh toffee on the edge of your chair is pretty well a faux pas.

Reading the Program Aloud: Not really necessary since everyone at the concert also has a program. Some of the people who weren't so cheap even have the one with all the color photographs. Reading the program silently but moving your lips is allowed, unless people are watching you closely. Folding the program into origami is out, unless you can do one of those lobsters in which case I'd like to talk to you privately after the performance.

Coughing: Ah well . . . it is a medical fact that quite a few people develop a cough when attending concerts. Laboratory studies with mice have failed to pinpoint the reason, but some theoretical material exists: the absence of light apparently stimulates the cough-nerve centres, or a little-understood but highly prevalent allergy exists in people, occasioned by the rubbing of bow on strings. This latter theory may have some credence when you consider that few people cough at band concerts; apparently, metal instruments don't bring about this reaction. Aha, say you sceptics, why then don't people cough at night in bed? Because they're asleep, of course! Falling asleep at a concert is a good way of preventing coughing. But it may give rise to snoring.

Some ways to overcome coughing include holding it in until there's a cymbal-crash from the percussionist. Here, timing is tricky, and again, a copy of the score is helpful. More drastic is not breathing at all until the end of the piece. The pitfalls of some symphonic works, particularly those of Anton Bruckner, are obvious.

If you find yourself to be one of those rare people blessed with an utter absence of these problems, you might wish to know what's available to combat them in others.

The most common is "shusshhhing." Less often used but more effective methods include hitting the offender, threatening her with a lawsuit as soon as the second movement is over, or setting fire to his tie with your Bic. Taking away the noise maker's box of chocolates and stomping on it is also a good move, as is hogging both armrests and repeatedly digging your elbow in just under the fourth rib. If none of these work, you might consider slipping the usher a fiver to call the offender away by claiming there's an error in his ticket and a motorcycle gang has just upturned his Tercel.

Finally, a couple of points to ponder on arrivals and departures. If there is music coming from the front of the concert hall and you are not yet in your seat, it's a safe bet you're late. People will have to get up, you'll trip over their feet, and the entire viola section will know what a klutz you are . . . no matter how much you may have tipped the attendant in the coat-check room.

The rule of thumb is this: so long as there's music being played, remain in your seat, unless the orchestra is playing "Jerusalem" during the Last Night of the Proms, or some really catchy dance number is being performed and the horn players are taking off their jackets and openly challenging the conductor.

Some symphonies have trick endings, so don't be fooled by any momentary silence into rushing for the foyer. If you wait at least three minutes, chances are good that the piece is over if nothing else happens. You may be alone in your seat by then, but no one would ever be able to accuse you of being rude or uncultured.

Now, as to what to eat during a concert. Even though some places sell chocolates, you shouldn't really eat them, especially not the kind with nuts in them. Soft centres are essential. Ideally, only soft food should be consumed at a concert. Bread sticks, celery, really fresh Macintosh apples, are all inopportune victuals. If you can't get through the evening without feeling faint, perhaps a bowl of baked custard or some yogurt concealed in your stole or under your jacket will help.

Finally, try to limit the number of charms on your bracelet to six or seven (you may wear more if they're plastic!) and wear loose, comfortable clothes of some nonstarched material. Transfer your parking change to your overcoat pocket before entering the performing hall proper.

If more people followed some of these simple, common-sense approaches, there would be fewer people like me leaning over the backs of their seats at a critical point during "Dance of the Sugarplum Fairies" and pushing a grapefruit into someone's face.

*P*lay Dominoes!

———————❧———————

*T*HE STUFF THAT'S GOING ON in restaurants these days — no, I mean around the food — is getting out of control. Fashion shows, no less. Scotch tastings. Photography exhibits. Meet-the-wine-maker-he's-from-Wisconsin dinners. Live music. *Arrgghh*!

Shouldn't this sort of thing be confined to the home? Or the mall? The gallery? The coffeehouse or the concert stage? Frank and Betty's house?

It's the threat of live entertainment that worries me most. Wasn't it George Bernard Shaw who answered, after being asked by a solicitous restaurateur, pointing to the ensemble of musicians in a corner of the restaurant, what Shaw would like the band to play: "Dominoes!"

When I go to a restaurant, which happens fairly often, I mostly go there to eat. Not all the time, true, but mostly. A little food, a little conversation, a little business maybe, but primarily food. On occasion, I go to use the telephone, wait for a friend, or get out of the rain, but by and large, food is what I'm after.

What I'm not after is a major confrontation, a heartfelt rendition of "The Streets of Laredo," a Houdiniesque experience with parts of my dinner, a blue-suited man with dandruff romping through "Flight of the Bumblebee" on a dime-store fiddle, blue carnations in a bushel basket or a rounded lady doing things with

169

her upper body that may be perfectly fine back home, around midnight at the oasis, but which probably would still be banned today in Blairmore.

Time was when eating in restaurants was all very much simpler. A jolly waitress who was somebody's mom brought you soup and crackers and wiped the table and complained about the weather. You had steak and chips, maybe half a bottle of Sparkling Indiscretion, and paid fifteen dollars for two. The waitress got a two-dollar tip and the whole world was in order.

No more. The waitress isn't destined to become anybody's mother, and the young waiter with the nine-inch hips is worse. The steak and chips have long disappeared under layers of sauce and seasoning, and a decent tinned carrot and peas is some sort of green thing of obscure origin enveloped in custard. The bill is $126 for two, and the tip has to run close to $25 if you want them to at least be civil the next time you come.

Of course, that all depends on whether they were civil the first time round.

Consider the work you go through to get to a restaurant for the food these days. First, there's the reservation. I generally call up and find myself talking to a machine.

"Bonjour. This is l'Auberge de Wetaskiwin," purrs a voice. "I am ver' sorry there is no one here to take your reservation in ze flesh . . ." One shudders, but the implacable machine grinds on. "Soon you will hear le tone, and zen you must leave your name, your number, the number of people in your party, your credit card expiry date, your licence number, two pieces of photo-identification which will be returned to you, and a deposit of $250. Someone will call you back to confirm, soon. Oh yes, specialities at l'auberge are soufflé au paprika, les omelettes de fenêtre, brown paper papillotes à la mystère, et l'oeufs foo yong." And so on.

Now the truth is, I do not want anyone to call me back about this. It's supposed to be a surprise. I just want to book a quiet table for two for Friday night, and I'll take my chances with the menu when I get there. The message goes on, finally comes the beep, but you know what's happened . . . they spent so much time talking on the endless tape that there's not enough time for your message. All you get out is your name and the thing recycles:

"Bonjour!" says le voix again. "This is l'Auberge . . .," and I smash the phone down and rip off a fingernail.

Still, off we go on Friday night, because someone had a cousin who once knew the sous-chef's dog trainer and they swear by the cuisine.

It is some of the famous nouvelle Californie cuisine. I was never too unhappy with any of the ancienne kind — Californie or otherwhere — but progress is progress even if it means the four pillars of nouveauté: goat cheese, leeks, sun-dried tomatoes, and polenta.

And no damned butter on my baked potato!

We get there, and while I find a place to park she — the lady who, this very evening, will be asked a major question — stands outside under an umbrella. When I get back, she wants to go home. It seems that several passing businessmen have asked her if she was doing anything this evening and the maître d' came out from l'Auberge and suggested she move along, this being a respectable neighborhood after all. I vow silently to kill the maître d'. Better still, I vow to do something that'll really hurt: not tip. The maître d' is the same one you've run into. He has one suit and he's worn it for the last seventeen years. He has a pudding-bowl haircut and a goatee, but an admittedly impressive accent. He sneers at you, at his list of names (they can never find Smith, you know; there's always trouble spelling it!), sneers at your coat and takes it as though it was just handed to him by Sir Walter Raleigh on a rainy night. You have a feeling you'll never see it again, or if you do it will have been chewed by a German shepherd named Rex.

The maitre d' assures you that your table is ready. It is, too, a charming, minuscule table in a thoroughfare right in the middle of the dining room. You suggest that you'd hoped for something more intimate. He tells you that this is the most intimate table they have. You wonder if the word hasn't lost a little in the translation since you used it last.

Here in Canada we don't fully seem to understand the meaning of the word *intimate*. Maybe it all has something to do with those wide open spaces we came here for. "Give me a secluded, intimate table," I say to the maitre d'. "Fine," he says, pocketing the yellow bill and marching me right next to a convention dinner of photocopier salesmen who are well into their fourth round of bar-Scotch-and-Fresca. Intimate that ain't.

So you complain ever so gently and they put you on the balcony where it's dark and quiet. This isn't nearly so generous a gesture as it first appears, since February in northern Alberta still carries a bit of a nip in the air. You might have to ask for your coat back after all. Never mind, soon the hot rolls and the chilled champagne will arrive. Or, as is often the case, vice versa.

The busboy is next to approach from the dim recesses of the restaurant. He puts a roll in the ashtray, drops the whipped butter into the candle, and sets the little bowl of celery right on the wee blue velvet box you brought to hand across the table at an opportune moment you're hoping to get.

The table almost always has one leg shorter than its companions. You ask for a matchbook from the people at the table next to you. It turns out the nice gentleman there speaks only Portuguese, and it takes some doing to convince him that you do not want to (a) take his salad, (b) question his choice of necktie, or (c) hit his wife. Finally, a waiter brings a matchbook and you lean down for a minute, the blood pounding in your head as you try to secure the table. You straighten up and your shoulder catches the edge of the table and a glass of ice water cascades into your companion's lap. She shrieks and says several things you had previously only found women saying in an Erica Jong book. People are now starting to stare, and you begin to wish you'd ordered in pizza and watched Pat and Vanna instead. The music comes on, and to your surprise, the world's only remaining functioning quadraphonic sound system is situated directly above your head. It looks as though there's going to be shouting, in competition with Edith Piaf, throughout dinner. Maybe this isn't the night for the proposal, after all. Writing it down? Impossible. Just try getting a piece of paper and a pen: the maître d' will be convinced you're a restaurant critic and then there could be even more trouble. Surreptitiously, you try to pocket the little package, only to find that there's vinaigrette over it, and a major oil slick is spreading all over the part that says "Birks."

You summon the maître d' and get into an argument over the table and the music. There's a sort of compromise: he'll turn the music down ("But I can tell you, Monsieur, it will make the chef very unhappy") and you resolve that not only is there not going to be any tip but you'll come around and slash his tires just as soon as you can find out where he lives. Why don't they have badge numbers you can ask for?

Then, the menu. Ah, yes, the menu. Or, as it is most often, Le menu. It's entirely in misspelled French, and you end up ordering by half pointing and half slurring your words and trying to cough at the same time so no one will notice you don't know how to say confit de canard or gâteau St. Honoré.

The wine steward arrives to offer a pleasant surprise: not only is he the father of the maître d' but he is pleased as punch to tell you that there's none of the $12 Beaujolais left. In fact, the only wine left costs $47.50. The first bottle is bad, naturally. Well, it happens sometimes. You just can't quite put your finger on it, but a light blue Chablis wants some further questioning. The cork is placed in the butter dish, and as you reach for it, to give it that knowing twist of the thumb and forefinger, it slips from your grasp, across the table and . . . well, you know that low-cut dress she was wearing that's been driving you crazy all evening? Uh-huh!

She sits bolt upright and makes a small choking sound. You try to find some proper way of offering to retrieve the cork, but the wine waiter has beaten you to it. The Portuguese gentleman from

173

the next table is now firmly convinced that there is something wrong here and leaps to your lady's defence, fish fork at the ready. There is shouting.

Of course, the music's turned up again to act as a diversion.

Finally comes the first course, and you can turn your attention to dinner. The soup — it's always onion soup — has these strings. You are about to enter into a long-lasting relationship with your soup. In fact, you end up being bound to it!

There is something about the extra pepper in restaurants, come salad time, that is getting entirely out of hand. Now, I figure if someone can't make a decent salad dressing with the right amount of pepper, he has no business in the kitchen of a hundred-dollar-per-person restaurant. And why only pepper? Just once, I'd like someone to ask me if I'd like more fresh shrimp in my salad. Anyway, foolishly you say yes to the extra pepper. A grinder the size of the CN Tower is stuck over your table. There are a couple of twists and you begin to sneeze.

And so it goes. The main course comes, and you don't recognize any of the vegetables, certainly not by color or shape or even smell. What could have been carrots in a previous life have been suspiciously topiaried into hearts and diamonds: for the first time in months, you're holding a flush, only it's right next to the roast beef.

The knives are out of order.

Ever a glutton for punishment, you opt for dessert, and some very cold sort of custard arrives with a kind of melted brown sugar on top. To try to save the day and just maybe refloat the idea around the little oil-stained package in your breast pocket, which set you back the limit on both charge cards, you order brandy.

It comes in an aquarium that has been in the oven for an hour. The stuff goes straight up your nose and you cough and snort for fifteen minutes. But you do get to it after a while, and by the time the coffee comes, it looks as though you might be able to linger a little after all. The place has emptied a bit, the music's down, the maître d' is off at half-time, and the two of you spend a lot of time looking across the table at each other. This, just as soon as you get rid of the glare from the little yellow knobby toad-like candle and once the plastic rose is out of the way so you won't knock it over if you reach across on impulse to take her hand.

Is this the moment?

Several people answer for you: the folk singer, the fiddler, the belly dancer. They're all here to delight and entertain. Right now! The folk singers tend to be young and they're the easiest to dispatch. As soon as they start in on "The Ballad of the Springhill Mine Disaster," you say something direct like: "Shut up or I'll set your kaftan on fire." It's crude, but it works. The gypsy fiddlers are really tough. They've heard and seen it all and aren't about to leave until you lay a fiver on them and request "Habanera." And don't get caught trying to ask them for obscure classics either. "Okay, how about Widor's Organ Symphony No. 5?" you suggest smugly. You get the only gypsy fiddler whose day job is transcribing all of Widor's works for solo violin. He's there at your table till long after midnight. Not only do you have to tip him, you have to cover his overtime.

The belly dancers are the most unsettling. Midway through my veal piccata I do not wish to have to come to terms with a lady throwing her torso about as though this were an Olympic event.

"How come you keep staring at her . . . top?" demands your companion. The lame excuse that it's only polite seems sadly lacking. Once again, you pocket the little blue package.

Finally, the bill.

"No, we don't take Amex." crows the maître d' triumphantly, and you have to borrow a couple of bucks. The Portuguese man has long since departed, and you turn to the only other possible source of funds. She slips you a twenty, but the moment is not comfortable.

Finally, your coats come back, covered in dew. You'll give the whole thing one last-ditch effort. The coats are placed on a chair, and you turn to your potential life's love to ask her a crucial question.

The lady with the flowers and the toys enters your life at that precise moment. She's the least sensitive of the lot that's gone before. She has no sense of timing, life, the real world — anything — ripped as she usually is on camomile tea. "No!" you shout emphatically and push past her, spilling her basket to the floor.

You leave her to the maître d' to deal with.

Outside in the night, it's raining again.

No, this isn't the evening to ask if she wants to come up for a nightcap. There'd probably be a break-in at your place around the time you got there!

So you head home alone and put on that nice Willie Nelson album and pour yourself a double Scotch before you turn out the lights.

Console yourself with this:

I once bought a round of blue carnations for a group of Japanese businessmen who were my guests at dinner, just to get rid of the flower lady. They smiled shakily and politely ate them. They did draw the line at the little stuffed doggies, though!

Mercifully, just then, the gypsy fiddler appeared and wanted to know if we would like something. "Yes," I said, "but you wouldn't be able to supply it." "Try me," he suggested. "Some way out of the fact that I can't speak Japanese and my guests don't speak English," I implored. Damn it all if he didn't start discussing Kurosawa films with my companions. In Japanese. Turns out he studied Suzuki violin there for years. Only restaurant fiddler I ever met who was helpful.

I still send him flowers every Christmas.

Cooking to Music: Notes on the Food of Love

---❦---

*T*his isn't as easy as it first appears. More than a matter of throwing on some Springsteen or the Vivaldi Seasons you've had since high school while the sauce separates. This means organizing, logic, programming.

The cats have seen it and heard it all before. They've crept out into the woods behind the house to root for truffles under the alders. (Misguided little creatures, let them have their Perigordian fantasies; I've got dinner to get to and it's just as well they're out from underfoot.)

Music for cooking, then, is it? All right, give me excess of it.

We will require more than a few pieces. There are whole sections to be accompanied, orchestrated: The Shopping, The Ritual Washing of a Week's Worth of Dishes, The *Mis-en-place-*ing, The Cooking Itself, The Eating, The After-Dinner Farrago, The Sending the Guests Home Humming, and The Next Morning, More.

Shopping's first, and most of what is heard in the mall, the stores, and the supermarkets is best ignored. Are there *still* The Hollyridge Strings, then?

Bringing personal sound with you by way of Mr. Sony's gift to perambulatory listening? Not for me. I get good gossip at the meat counter, and I want to hear the warning prespray hiss of the magic misters in the vegetable section just before I reach for the parsley. Less of a shock.

On the way home, in the car, is the time to set the concert in motion. I still think there is nothing better for it than The Travelling Wilburys. Yes, even now, after how many months has it been and poor Roy leaving us and all. Or the O'Kanes.

Everything into the house, piled on the counter, out of the way as I Do the Dishes. I *like* to do the dishes. Lots of them at a time. Manually. Many of my best thoughts come all Archimedean when I'm up to my elbows in the sink.

Suds soothe and focus the mind. There is warm water, lemony bubbles and mindless, easy activity to free the thoughts for exploration.

"Like a mantra?" I asked once.

"You're soaking in it," said Marge

Now to the prepping: *mis en place*, that sensible French term for "everything where it should be and ready to roll." I can't cook until it is all lined up in front of me, sometimes even pre-measured. For that I need music. Electric folk is a favorite: Fairport Convention, Steeleye Span, Silly Wizard, and Relativity. Mostly English, Scottish, Irish bands; once in a while Canadian — Rare Air being about the best. Oldies work too, for a surface-flush of nostalgia while you peel the peppers or chop the onion. When was the last time you cried to The Royal Teens' "Believe Me"?

Comes the cooking itself and there has to be music that sustains its own energy and thereby mine, as I leap about the kitchen, hacking away at things, often — involuntarily — parts of myself. Now is the time for music that provides appropriate underpinnings to ameliorate frustration when, as is always the case, there is no cinnamon whatsoever. The cats used it all up last Sunday, for toast in bed.

Trio jazz works perfectly: old Ray Bryant ("It's Madison Time . . ." I never could understand the "instructions" that were the lyrics, could you?), or *new* Ray Bryant, for that matter, still sounding superb. Oscar Peterson, Lance Hayward, some of the not-quite-so-moody-broody-icy ECM albums. Stuff with long, loping melodies, preferably loosely built on blues. Good 104-bar bass solos if the volume is sufficient, and a little brushwork on the drums.

No drum solos. Sorry, there's no place in my life for drum solos. This, from a fellow who once played drums in a country dance band? Now, *cowbell* work and we're talking. How else do you do a schottische, then?

While cooking, I need music that is familiar or at least predictable. I often play along in the kitchen where there are so any things lying about that can double as drumsticks — spoons, knives, celery, chopsticks. Probably best, chopsticks. I grew so fond of paradiddling with them that I took some into a recording studio once for the brief and not-much-lamented career of The Dorchester Rhythm Band.

Gzowski played us!

I also like to sing along. *Sing* may not be the appropriate term; for this, blues, doo-wop pop, and melodies of the mushbucket/Danny Boy persuasion are best. For this reason I would rather not have anyone else in the kitchen when I cook. Preferably not even in the house. Go and see what the cats have found under the alders. That way, my singing — not always in a readily known key — and the music it is meant to augment can both be very loud.

Curiously, perhaps, I am totally silent in the shower, although I do like to read here, trying to scan the major stories in the newspaper in the twenty seconds before it reverts to the pulp from whence it came. You see, it really *isn't* singing. It's back-of-the-throat, closed-mouth intense, rhythmic humming. It startles passersby. People are prone to it without being aware of it while wearing headphones, forgetting that other people can hear then. Next time you're watching a comedy on the plane, take your headphones off and listen to the ambient sound. Very weird, when two hundred people are in the same audio-mode.

When the food is finally cooking itself, the pace slows. This is the time for dizzy harp sonatas, lute tunes at least four centuries old, a bit of pre-Romantic piano tinkling. Even — I'm not at all ashamed to admit this — some of the more tuneful new age bits, such as Eric Tingstad, Nancy Rumbel, Spencer Brewer — the Beaux Arts Trio of new age.

This is also the point when the cook's bottle of wine veers dangerously close to E. Critical decision to be made: will he open another, thereby running risk of depleting the available supply for the guests and having to rummage about with a flashlight under the stairs to find some emergency Yago and cobweb-spraying it with Antique-in-a Drum, or switch to beer?

If the cooking has been going well, no major crises have developed, nothing has stuck to anything, the smoke alarm remained silent, not a lot of blood was drawn, and there is good, bubblesome action in the stove and on top of it — if the music has so far soothed the savage whatevers — there is no need to open more wine just yet. A cold, carefully built beer is nice.

Santa Fe Pale Ale is my favorite right now, but that needs a jaunt to New Mexico first. Calgary's Big Rock Porter is always in the cupboard, room temperature of course, along with Okanagan Springs Wheat Beer from Vernon, B.C., Tenpenny from Halifax, cold can of Keith's.

Here is where chamber music comes in, if it wants to. Never anything too familiar or too demanding. No major symphonies, no cathartic piano concertos by tormented Russian composers. Not the Trout Quintet, either. That's driving music, anyway — 190 on the clock and still in third. I always want two tape decks in the car at that point, for instant change — one for the Trout the other for the K.T. Oslin with "Hey Bobby" on it.

Comfort music. No minor keys. Hummability factor. The idea behind humming while cooking is that you don't want to hum whole bits, just monotonal lines, fragments. We're looking for

Arensky trios, Miaskovsky sonatas, some Philip Glass bits from *The Photographer*, Dowland ayres, Keith Jarrett who even does the humming for you.

At last, dinner. Now what? Nothing. Now I want to enjoy my food and my guests. Or my James Crumley or Elmore Leonard if I've prepared it all just for myself — also a particular pleasure worth exploring. I've been out in the kitchen, singing and working and humming and slicing and playing "Big Noise from Winnetka" on the Tupperware all afternoon. *Now* I want to chat with you, hear silly stories, laugh a lot, pour more wine — and not hear music. Worst of all is well-meaning, even well-playing, live musicians at the dinner table, playing while you try to eat. Whatever cretinous king first had that idea deserves the fact that he's only history now.

After dinner and we're talking — or not, if we did enough at table. The music gets trotted out in dumpsterloads; the Farrago takes shape. Old Bonzo Dog Band tracks; Neil Young's "Tonight's the Night"; The Hilliard Ensemble's "Pleugh Song"; Bakersfield Boogie Boys; Michael Hedges's "Aerial Boundaries"; Jonathan and Darlene Edwards; Captain Beefheart's harmonica on the "Strictly Personal" album; the last part of John Adams's "Grand Pianola Music"; George Jones's "Yabba-Dabba Do."

Maybe the Sunrise part of *The Gurrelieder* (but that's Schoenberg, they wonder); Billy Barber's first solo album on DMP; the incredible "La Folia" by Gregorio Paniagua and the loony Atrium Musicae de Madrid; Johnny Hartman, just to keep perspective on what singing is all about; the whole "Electric V" — all four sides or two CDs.

Bad blues by Kevin Coyne and Siren; Bahamian gospel by Joseph Spence; Wanda Landowska pounding that Pleyel harpsichord in traditional Polish wedding dances; Spike Milligan's "When the Lads Come a-Marching"; Alan Hovhaness's wonderful "Mysterious Mountain" — the Reiner/Chicago Symphony recording.

And speaking of mountains, a blast of Leslie West's "Mississippi Queen" at bloodletting volume around a quarter to one, just as people are out on the porch getting ready to find their cars.

If it all sounds familiar, you've probably had dinner at my house. Or, I want to come and have dinner at yours.

And in the morning? Sunday breakfast music means baroque trumpets and crashing choruses, the louder and the brighter the better, and I hope you slept well. In an hour or two, time to go back into the kitchen and do it again.

All the music's still there for it.

Cooking is an old jazz club term for everything *happening* on the stand at a session. When I played a little coffeehouse jazz on my old Kay upright — my duties also included keeping the espresso machine from exploding — thirty-something years ago, the Phantom Clarinetist came to the club one Sunday night.

Maybe he was St. Cecilia, the muse in street-guise, come to check up. Whatever, he came only the one time, so I guess my music-performing career wasn't meant to be. But that night, we were cooking — just the two of us, all but outnumbering the customers on one of those rainy Vancouver Sundays. Never found out his name. Espresso machine didn't blow up that night either.